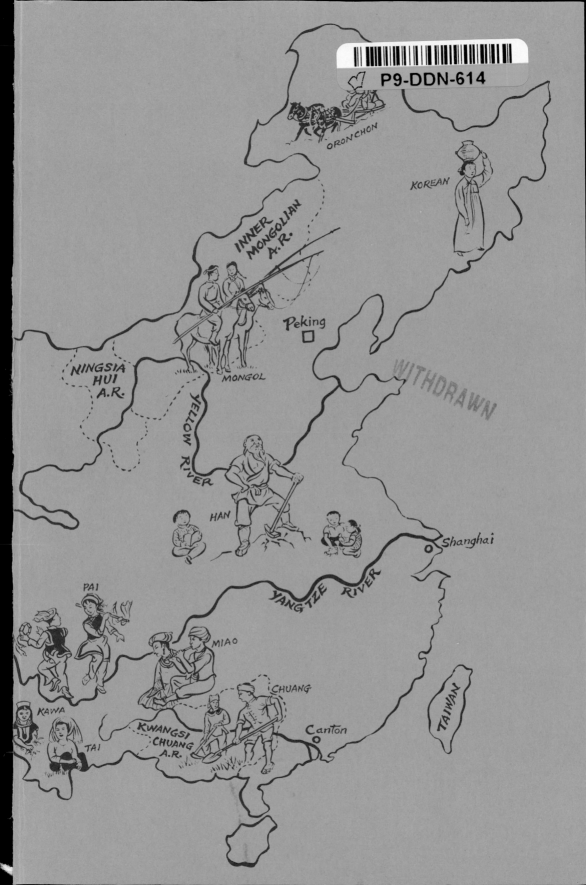

THE
MAGIC
BOAT AND
OTHER
CHINESE
FOLK
STORIES

ILLUSTRATIONS BY

# THE MAGIC BOAT AND OTHER CHINESE FOLK STORIES

by M.A. JAGENDORF
and VIRGINIA WENG

THE VANGUARD PRESS

NEW YORK

WAN-GO WENG

# CONTENTS

# ILLUSTRATIONS

ix

# FOREWORD

Folklore, folk tales are the treasure house of the world's stories. They are the common language of the world's literature. Every land, every people—all have them. And often the tales of different peoples, though thousands of miles apart, are the same in theme and plot. This "sameness" often points to a common origin. The unkind stepmother, the wise son and the stupid one, all kinds of folk are alike in folk tales the world over.

There is a common bond of friendly understanding in folk tales that knows not distance, creed, or color. Here all have a kinship of hopes, dreams, and desires. In these tales can be found a true brotherhood of mankind—a unity we hope will someday be realized.

*M. A. Jagendorf*

# INTRODUCTION

## THE CHINESE ARE NOT ALL ALIKE

When the words "China" and "Chinese" are mentioned, most persons think of a vast land inhabited by millions of people who all look alike, speak the same language, wear the same clothes, and eat the same foods. This is true to a certain extent, since of the total Chinese population, now estimated at over 950 million, 94 percent are "Han," or ethnic, Chinese. But the other 6 percent belong to minority nationalities. This may seem a low percentage, but, translated into numbers, it is more than 55 million people—about one-quarter of the population of the United States and more than that of all of France! Who are these minorities? They may be Turkic shepherds and grape growers in Sinkiang, nomadic horsemen in Inner Mongolia, Tungusic hunters and fishermen among the frigid mountains and rivers of Manchuria, Tibetan yak herders and farmers high in the Himalayas, or barefooted aborigines in the lush tropical lands of the southwest and south. They have their own distinctive cultures and identities, deeply influenced by the Han Chinese and contributing to the Han culture in return.

Even the majority Han, who share a common language and a history dating back some four thousand years, differ a great deal from one another. In the north, with Peking as center, the people have high cheekbones and are fairly tall. They speak *p'u-t'ung-hua*, also called "Mandarin," which has been adopted as the national language taught in all the schools. It is cold and dry in north China, and the staples are wheat, corn, and millet; northerners eat a great deal of noodles, dumplings, pan-fried bread, and steamed buns. With nomadic shepherds as neighbors, they are fond of lamb. They have a reputation for being frank and polite.

Farther south, the Chinese who live in the Yangtze River Delta, including the coastal city of Shanghai, are known for their creativity and shrewdness. They have produced many scholars, artists, and writers since the 13th century. They speak a *wu* dialect, which is faster and choppier than Mandarin, and their main food is rice, grown in paddies irrigated by many streams and rivers and plenty of rain. Fish, shrimp, chicken, duck, and pork are their favorites, but they cannot stand the sight or smell of unfamiliar lamb.

Still farther south, in Kwangtung Province, the capital of which is Canton, the people speak a melodious *yüeh* dialect, the one many Americans have heard in the Chinese sections of their cities. The weather is hot and humid, and the Cantonese are night owls who stay up late to enjoy the cooler hours. Their main food is also rice, but the Cantonese diet is probably the most varied in meats and vegetables and includes tropical fruits such as pineapples, lichees, and coconuts as well as large amounts of sea food. In complexion, these southerners are generally darker than their northern neighbors. They are said to be fiercely loyal and rather quick-tempered. Adjoining Kwangtung is Fukien Province, where the *min* dialect is spoken. The coastline of Fukien is irregular and dotted with islands, encouraging the Fukienese to be adventurous seafarers and traders. They settled Taiwan and are found in large numbers in southeast Asia and the Philippines. The Cantonese, too, are venturesome. They were the first Chinese to come to America.

Why are the Chinese so different from one another and

where did all these minority nationalities—Turks, Mongols, Tibetans, and others—come from? Of course, geography, climate, and history played important parts in creating regional differences. Although the Chinese believed from ancient times that they belonged to a "Central Kingdom" and called outsiders "barbarians," their first few dynasties consisted of kingdoms and dukedoms at war with one another, and they did not become a united empire until the Ch'in dynasty (221 B.C.–206 B.C.), which is generally believed to have given the country the name "China." Later, during the glorious Han dynasty (202 B.C.–220 A.D.), the empire expanded westward to Chinese Turkistan, eastward to Korea, and southward to Vietnam. After this period, the Chinese liked to call themselves "Han people."

In the brilliant T'ang dynasty (618 A.D.–907 A.D.), China was the greatest power in the East, and further explorations of the western regions were made, adding new alien territories to Chinese domination. Vast trade and cultural exchanges took place, attracting floods of visitors and immigrants from neighboring and distant lands. Between those long and stable reigns, China was weak and disunited, and it was frequently invaded and overrun by barbarians, some of whom enjoyed the "Central Kingdom" so much that they stayed. Twice China fell completely under foreign rule. The invincible Mongols occupied the country for nearly one hundred years during the Yüan dynasty (1279 A.D.–1368 A.D.), bringing Central Asian administrators and military forces. Manchu emperors sat on the dragon throne for almost three hundred years and became so Chinese themselves that in the end they could not be distinguished from the natives. Their dynasty, called Ch'ing (1644 A.D.–1911 A.D.) was the last imperial rule before China became a republic—first under the Nationalists and now under the Communists. It is easy to see how, as time went on, China became dotted with enclaves of minorities and added to its territory large areas populated mostly by non-Han people. Furthermore, there has always been a natural mingling of populations with neighboring countries along the long boundary line.

The People's Republic of China, recognizing the importance of minority nationalities, has designated five autonomous regions: the Tibetan Autonomous Region (inhabited by Tibetans); the Sinkiang Uighur Autonomous Region (inhabited by

Uighurs and other Central Asians such as the Kazakhs); the Ningsia Hui Autonomous Region (inhabited by Chinese muslims called Hui); the Kwangsi Chuang Autonomous Region (inhabited mainly by a large minority called the Chuang) and the Inner Mongolian Autonomous Region (inhabited by Mongolians). Many other minorities also live in smaller autonomous districts or counties among the Han in regular provinces or within the five large autonomous regions.

There is no satisfactory way to classify Chinese ethnic groups. The Chinese government lists 54 minorities in addition to the Han majority. One way to group them is according to languages since they belong to four separate language families: Sino-Tibetan, Altaic, Austroasiatic, and Indo-European, but the last two groups are very small.

Certain minorities have their own written languages; for example, the Koreans, Mongols, Tibetans, Manchus, and Uighurs. But the Manchus have nearly all given up studying or using their own writing. A few minorities have inadequate written languages that the Chinese government is trying to help perfect, while others have no written languages at all and need to develop new ones. The purpose for promoting reading and writing is, of course, to spread education and ideology.

Besides fighting illiteracy, the government also tries to raise the standard of living among minority groups through health care and economic development. Instead of trying to make them adopt the Han culture, the government works with ethnic leaders and gives the minorities some self-rule, encouraging them to keep their own customs, dress, and culture. At the same time, young people are being educated in Chinese schools such as the Central Institute for National Minorities, with the hope that someday all the people will be integrated. Han children are also being taught to be aware of other ethnic groups.

Folk tales were collected from all over China in the 1950s and 1960s, but the Cultural Revolution that began around 1966 interrupted this work. However, many stories had already been published. Using available sources, we have chosen 33 tales from 21 ethnic groups, including the Han and 20 minorities, and adapted them for American readers. The stories are chosen first for their quality and, second, as representative of diverse groups, though certainly not of all of them.

We were obliged to translate non-Han names from the Chinese rather than from the original languages. Names for plants and animals are often regional folk names, differing markedly from standard or scientific terms. As far as possible, our translations are based upon Chinese encyclopedias and dictionaries. For illustrations, the artist, Wan-go Weng, used publications from China as references for scenes and costumes.

We hope our readers will enjoy these stories and find it interesting to learn about the variety of people who live in China. The Chinese are all "People of the Central Kingdom," but they are not all alike!

*Virginia Weng*

# HAN

漢

# ERH-LANG
# AND THE SUNS

HAN

漢

In the time before anything and everything, there were Seven Suns in the land of China. They shone without end and there was neither day nor night. People suffered cruelly from the heat and the never-ending blinding light. They could not farm their land or rest in peace because of the fierce burning glare. If they put a blob of newly kneaded dough on top of the courtyard wall, it would bake to a crisp and turn into a chunk of charcoal in no time at all!

Now, among the people there was a very strong young man named Erh-lang. Erh-lang was stronger than fifty men. He could lift mountains with his hands and would fling great rock boulders to the sky just to show how strong he was. Everyone admired him.

One day the wise men came together to speak of the terror of the Seven Suns. Said one of the wise men: "Let us

3

ask Ehr-lang to help us in our sad trouble. He is the only one who can conquer these blinding, blistering Suns."

Everyone thought this a good idea, and seven of the oldest men were sent to ask Erh-lang for help.

When they came to him, he was rolling giant gray boulders along the dry land.

"We have come to you, Erh-lang," the oldest said, "to beg you to rid us of the terrible plague in our land. I speak of the Seven Suns that blind us with their light and burn us with their heat."

"I know how you suffer," said Erh-lang, "for I, too, am troubled by their never-ending burning and never-ending light. I will gladly help you, and I will start at once."

The old men thanked him and wished him luck.

Erh-lang kept his word. He began by watching the Seven Suns carefully. Soon he noticed that they did not come up together, but that they followed one upon the other.

"That is fine," he thought. "Getting one at a time will be much easier."

He walked up to a rocky mountain nearby and slowly tilted it to one side, leaving a deep hole in the earth. Then he waited for a Sun to rise. Soon it came out of the east, filling the sky and land with glaring light. Erh-lang dashed up, spread his huge arms wide, took hold of the giant hot Sun, and, rushing to the mountain he had tilted sideways, threw the Sun into the hole underneath. Holding down the Sun with his giant boot, he pushed the mountain on top of it.

"Now there is one less burning glare. That was easy. I'll get ready for the next Sun."

He looked around and saw another big, rocky mountain, rolled it aside, leaning it carefully on its own weight, again making a deep hole in the earth.

He rested and waited. After a time, the heat and light told of the coming of the next Sun. No sooner was it out from the east than Erh-lang leaped at it, got hold of it with his gigantic arms, and flung it into the hole under the mountain. Holding down this Sun, too, with his giant boot, he dragged the mountain over it and covered it.

"Now two of these misery-makers are gone," he said, waving his arms in the air. He rested for a time and then he raised another mountain, caught another Sun, and buried it. He did this to three other Suns until there was just one left.

Now, the Seventh Sun had seen what had happened to his six brothers. He had seen one after another disappear and he was greatly worried. He was almost afraid to climb out of the east.

In the end he did. Cautiously and slowly, he crept up . . . and, seeing a plant nearby, hid under it, hoping Erh-lang would not see him. But Erh-lang did see him, for the Seventh Sun could not hide his light or his heat.

Erh-lang had pushed aside a mountain to bury Seventh Sun. Now he rushed up, ready for his task. But Seventh Sun began to weep and begged, "Please don't bury me under the mountain, powerful Erh-lang, as you have my brothers. I will stop giving terrible heat and blinding light. Only don't bury me under the mountain."

People had gathered around Erh-lang. They felt sorry for Seventh Sun and joined in the begging.

"Be kind, Erh-lang," pleaded Seventh Sun.

"I will not bury you, Seventh Sun, if you promise to shine for only a part of the day so that the people can rest without your heat and your awful glare the rest of the time."

"I promise, I swear," cried Seventh Sun, "I swear, only don't bury me under the mountain."

Erh-lang's heart had softened, as had the hearts of the people.

"I know you will keep your promise," said Erh-lang, "and so I will not bury you."

Erh-lang let Seventh Sun come up from under the plant to give light and warmth to the people during the day.

And since the light and heat were not there all the time, for the Sun would set by nightfall, it was a benefit to all—both to the earth and to man.

Ever since then, the Seventh Sun would not harm the plant that had given him shelter. No matter how long that plant is in the sunshine, it does not dry up. Folks call it "Water-Leaf Plant" (*shui-yeh-ts'ai*), for it is always lush, green, and soft. And to this day it is still the people's favorite wild-growing vegetable.

# THE CHAO KU BIRD

HAN

漢

In the ancient, ancient days in China, when men and creatures and all nature worked happily together, an old woman lived with her daughter and with the wife of her son who had died in the wars. She loved her daughter very much and gave her the best food she had and silk for her clothes. But she was mean and unkind to her daughter-in-law. She always made her do the hardest work in the house, gave her rags for clothes and left-overs for food, and there was little of that. But the two young girls—they were nearly the same age—loved each other and called each other sister.

The daughter did no end of kind deeds for her brother's young widow. They were always together. The old mother did not like this, but she could do nothing about it.

One day she gave the daughter-in-law a basket. "Go

into the hills near the big mountain and gather all the mulberry leaves you can to feed our silkworms," she said.

The young woman went into the hills, searching for mulberry leaves all day long. Toward the end of the day she had only a few; she just could not find many. She sat down by the mountain path and cried her heart out, for she did not know what to do and dared not go home.

Meanwhile, her sister-in-law waited and waited for her, wondering what had happened. "She must be tired and hungry, perhaps she is lost," thought the daughter. So she took some bread and soup and millet gruel and went up the hills to look for her sister-in-law. She looked a long time and finally found her sitting by the road, weeping.

"It is so late, and you are still here," said the daughter.

"I am afraid to go home. Your mother will be angry with me and might beat me. I found hardly any mulberry leaves. I will sleep here for the night. I am not afraid and I shall find enough berries to eat. Tomorrow I will look again for mulberry leaves; maybe I will be lucky and find more then."

"But you must be hungry. Look, I have brought you bread, soup, and millet gruel, and I have come to help you." She persuaded her sister-in-law to take a few bites and drink some of the soup. Then, since it was still light, they both set out to look for mulberry leaves. They looked and looked, but still they could not find any more, only dry branches and brambles.

The daughter-in-law begged: "Sister, please go home. It is getting dark and wild animals will soon come out for their food. Let me look alone for another hour or so. Perhaps the Spirit of the Mountain will take pity on me and turn these dry branches and brambles into mulberry trees."

But the daughter refused. "Yes, tigers and wolves will soon come out, but I will not go home without you. I shall stay with you and help you." They searched all the evening, walking as far as the mountain. Night came and the moon rose, but they did not have any luck. Both girls were tired and discouraged.

Spoke the daughter sadly: "Spirit of the Mountain, come to our aid and help us find mulberry leaves. If you do, I will even marry you."

At these words, a warm strong whirlwind came up, and when it stopped—lo! the whole mountain was covered with beautiful mulberry trees. The girls were very happy to see this wonder, and they picked a full basket and went home.

There the old woman was wild with worry for her daughter. When she saw her, she was overjoyed, but she scolded the young widow for having made her sister-in-law follow her into the hills.

The next day the old woman again sent the daughter-in-law out to look for mulberry leaves. The other girl followed, and they came back with full baskets. Again and again the two friends went up the hills, coming back with food for the silk-worms.

One day, as the girls were in their garden, the sky sud-denly grew dark and a black whirlwind descended. The daugh-ter-in-law turned to the daughter to talk to her, but she was not there.

She had disappeared without a sign. The Spirit of the Mountain who had accepted her offer of marriage had taken her in the wind to his home in the mountain.

The young widow was very unhappy, for she loved her sister-in-law very much. "I cannot live without her," she said, running everywhere to look for her.

She did not go home, but kept on looking the next day and the next night, crying for her sister all the time, stumbling over the rocks until the soles of her shoes wore out. Her clothes were torn to tatters by the brambles.

The birds in the forest took pity on her and threw their feathers at her. Soon she was covered with feathers. The next day the north wind blew and winter was upon the land, but she had turned into a bird, a bird ever flying around and crying *"chao ku! chao ku!* Looking for Sister! Looking for Sister!"*, searching for her sister-in-law.

To this day you can hear the cry of *chao ku! chao ku!* The young widow-bird is still looking for her lost sister-in-law, her friend.

# THE GREAT DEEDS OF KING YÜ

HAN

漢

In the endless years that have no beginning and no end, there lived in China a great king named Yü. Many tales are told of his great exploits, but none was greater than how he directed the flow of waters from the sky and how he built gray mountains and tall peaks.

King Yü was truly a king of the people. With his great strength he worked day and night to serve them. He had calloused hands and wore straw shoes on his feet. His face was deeply tanned by the rays of the sun and was as dark as a black *kuo*.*

One day he looked around his beloved land and noted that the hot sun always rose in the east of the Heaven.

The king said to his ministers, "I must make the wa-

* A *kuo* (called a wok in America by the Chinese immigrants from Canton) is an iron curved-bottom frying pan that turns black with use.

ters flow to the east, where the burning sun always rises, for the heat is so great there that no man can live, nor any crops grow. I must direct the floods in that direction so that they will not drown anyone or cause any harm to plants." He set to work at once.

Seeing that there were floods in the south, he decided to move some boulders to stop them. First he pushed the giant rocks, which lay in heaps, apart. He piled them in baskets, which he carried on the ends of his shoulder pole. In three days and three nights he moved ninety loads from T'ai Shan, the highest mountain in Shantung. The ninety loads made nine great piles, which stopped the floods in the south. They stand high and mighty against the blue sky and form nine sections of a new mountain range. The Chinese call these the Long White Mountains.

Then the king spoke to his people: "Now I must make separate, deep river beds through which the waters will flow easily."

He spoke magic words and there came up first one of the giant dragons of the land. He was blue in color and his scales glowed in the sun. His four feet were each as big as great trees, ending in sharp claws. A straggling green beard hung from his chin and he had a long coiling tail. He breathed mists and clouds as he twisted and turned his giant body in all directions. Great geysers of water rushed from his nostrils.

Following the dragon was a giant snake so long you could not see his end. His tongue, thick and narrow, darted and moved in his open mouth.

Spoke King Yü to the mist-breathing dragon, "Dig a ditch beside these mountains for the waters to flow to the east." Then he turned to the snake and said, "You, too, must make a deep bed on the other side through which the waters will flow in the right direction." Then he left them to do their work.

The dragon began at once. He dug his claws in, right and left, flinging earth and stones in all directions. He moved his body this way and that way and soon he made a deep bed through which the waters would flow easily.

The giant snake was lazy. He just rolled around, this way and that way, making only a shallow depression in the earth.

"That is good enough," hissed the giant Snake, "I am tired of working."

"My ditch is deeper," roared Dragon, "it is better than yours."

"Mine is good enough," hissed Snake. "Besides, I finished first." And then, hissing with all his might so he could be heard far away, he zished, "I am finished, King Yü. I am finished."

"I am also finished, Great King Yü," Dragon bellowed so that the boulders shook and trembled.

Far away in his house, sitting on a stone boulder he had rolled in, King Yü heard them hissing and roaring.

"Good," he shouted, "I will come to see what you two have done."

He came to the mountain and saw the deep ditch Dragon had dug with his giant claws.

"You have made a good place for the river," King Yü said, "and I will reward you for your fine work. I will put you into the Heaven, where you will direct the rains to the earth for the growth of grain and trees and flowers and plants."

So King Yü put the dragon into the sky and there he has been ever since, sending life-giving water to the earth for the benefit of man and land.

Then King Yü turned to see what the snake had done and saw the shallow wide depression he had made by merely rolling from side to side a few times.

"Shame on you, Snake, for making such a shallow bed for a river! For this I order you to stay for the rest of time in the deep ocean where the ever-beating waves will pound you without stopping. That will be your punishment for making such a poor water bed."

And so it happened; the snake was put into the ocean and the dragon into the sky.

Then King Yü ordered the water to flow through the river beds made by the dragon and the snake. He was pleased at the sight.

"Perhaps it would be good to have two giant peaks beyond the Long White Mountains," he said. He took off his straw shoes and emptied the sand and dust in them on the ground. The two piles grew into two tall yellow peaks beyond the Long White Mountains, and there they have been ever since.

This is just one of the tales they tell of King Yü, the hero who lived in ancient China. There are many more.

# THE TALE OF THE SHRIMP AND THE EARTHWORM

HAN

漢

L isten to a tale of very ancient days folks tell in China.

In those days, the shrimp and the earthworm lived and walked around the earth like all other animals.

The earthworm had big, round eyes to see the world around him and to help him find food. He was a happy fellow and he loved to sing.

The shrimp in his strong shell-covering had no eyes. He was blind. He did not see the golden sun or silver moon, he did not see the stars in Heaven or the flowers and trees of the earth. He was always stumbling around, trying to find something to eat. His was a sad life.

He longed to see what the world was like, so he went to the earthworm crawling all over and said, "Please lend me your big, round eyes so I can see the world just once. I would be satisfied with just one little look."

The earthworm felt sorry for the blind shrimp, so he took his big shiny eyes and put them on the shrimp's pointy head.

The shrimp was happy and excited. Now he saw the world for the first time. He saw the blue sky and the golden sun, he saw the trees bending with the wind, and many stars in the sky.

"If only I could keep these eyes, how happy I would be," he said to himself, and he leaped into the water!

The earthworm kept on calling the shrimp to return his eyes, but the shrimp pretended not to hear him; he was happily swimming around looking at the fishes and everything in the water.

Since that time the poor earthworm has been crawling around on the earth trying to find the shrimp who took his eyes, while the shrimp is happily swimming around with the borrowed eyes.

And it has been like that ever since: the earthworm crawling around blind looking for the shrimp who borrowed his eyes. He became so sad that he stopped singing.

But of course the earthworm's eyes do not fit the shrimp, and that is why the shrimp's eyes look even bigger and more bulging than when they belonged to the earthworm.

# THE
# SAD
# END OF
# WU-LING-TZU

HAN

漢

One day many years ago, there was great excitement among the birds of China. It was the birthday of the King of Birds, and all the feathered subjects had been invited to a grand party to honor the day.

Every bird put on the best feathers he had—all except one: the bird called Wu-ling-tzu,* who was as bare as a tree in wintertime.

He had no feathers and was always cold and shivering.

"I have no feathers. My skin is blue and I am always cold—so cold." He kept on crying without end, until the King of Birds heard him and felt sorry for him. He sent out an

---

* We do not know what kind of bird the Wu-ling-tzu was. The reference to its nakedness is mystifying, for although all birds molt, they do not shed all their feathers at once. Only the common chicken sometimes loses all its feathers.

19

order to all the birds for each to give Wu-ling-tzu one feather.

All the birds quickly obeyed and soon Wu-ling-tzu had as many beautiful feathers as if he were a prince dressed for his wedding day. He looked magnificent, and all the birds admired him.

Wu-ling-tzu heard the praises and they filled his little head with pride and conceit.

"Truly, I am beautiful," he cried, "More beautiful than any bird. Only the royal phoenix can equal my beauty. And I am not even sure of that."

He kept on talking this way without stopping, and the other birds got tired of his bragging chatter. The King, too, became annoyed at the silly boasting of Wu-ling-tzu.

"Now he thinks he is better than all of us," cried the birds indignantly.

"We shall teach him a lesson he will never forget," the birds decided. "Let us fly to that silly Wu-ling-tzu and each take back the feather we gave him."

The birds all flew around Wu-ling-tzu, and soon he was bare and naked again. The blowing wind made his skin turn as blue as it had been before, and he shivered with cold.

Silly Wu-ling-tzu never was given any feathers again, and has remained cold and shivering to this day as a punishment for his boasting and bragging.

# THE MAGIC BOAT

HAN

漢

Han folk, like folk everywhere in the world, after the day's hard work and their simple meal, sit around and talk. They talk of this and that and often they tell tales of what happened in the good old days.

In those good old days there lived a woodcutter named Wang. He was a good man and worked hard to support himself and his old mother.

One day, as he was walking home from work in the hills, a load of dry branches on his back, he came to a wide river over which there was a narrow wooden bridge for crossing. As he got near the bridge he saw an old man on it. The old man had just reached the middle when a gust of wind flung him to the side. He lost his balance and fell into the wildly rushing water below and began battling to reach the bank. But he was not strong enough.

Wang threw down his back pack and leaped into the river. He was strong and with a few strokes reached the struggling old man and, holding him, swam to the bank. The old man was half frozen and trembling from the cold, so Wang put him on his back and took him to the old man's home. The man thanked Wang again and again for having saved his life.

After they dried themselves and rested a while, the old man took out a little wooden box from under his bed and said, "I thank you for your help and good heart. Such kindness should be well rewarded." He slid open the top of the box and drew out a little paper boat. "See this little boat. I shall give it to you as a token of my gratitude."

Wang looked at the paper boat. It was complete in every way, with a covered bunk for sleeping, oars, rudder, and anchor.

"Dear friend," the old man said, "This is not a child's toy, it is a magic boat that will save your life as you saved mine. Take it, and take good care of it."

Wang took the boat as the old man continued, "Soon a great flooding rain will come here and your paper boat will turn into a great wooden boat where you will be safe. You can take into it as many animals as you wish, but do not take any man on it. If you do, it will bring you harm."

The old man again thanked Wang; then they bade each other good-by.

Holding the boat carefully, the woodcutter picked up his load of wood and started home. No sooner did he reach there than it began to rain. Thunder shook his walls and lightning flashed all around. It rained for many days without stopping. The water rose to the threshold of Wang's house. Wang and his mother were frantic. Then he suddenly remembered the paper boat in the wooden box, which he had hidden in a crack in the wall. He took out the box and put the boat on the water. It immediately turned into wood and began to grow bigger and bigger. In a short time it was a full-size river-going boat. Wang and his mother got in. The wind

swished the rain in all directions. Animals appeared every-where, struggling in the water: snakes, animals with fur, even bees and ants. They all swam around the boat and Wang and his mother took them up as fast as they could.

Suddenly Wang heard someone shouting, "Wang! Wang! Help! Save me!"

Wang looked and there was Chang, the son of one of the rich men of the village. Wang forgot the warning of the old man and stretched out an oar and helped Chang get onto the boat.

The rain continued for a long time. Then it stopped and the boat touched dry land. Everyone was glad to leave.

When they were gone, the boat began shrinking and again became a paper boat, which Wang put back into the little box for safekeeping.

Chang looked in astonishment at the change. Then he spoke, "Truly this is a magic boat! Where did you get it, Wang?"

"An old man whom I saved from drowning gave it to me."

"You are a lucky man, Wang, to have such a wonderful magic boat. Why not give it to the Emperor? He would surely reward you richly for such a marvelous gift."

"I cannot go to the capital to see the Emperor! I must stay here and work to support my old mother."

"Let me go with the boat instead and I will tell the Emperor that you sent it to him. Then I will come back and tell you what reward he has given to you. Maybe you will be made a minister and live with your mother in a mansion."

"Go, good friend Chang. I will wait here for the glad news," said Wang.

So Chang went to the palace with the little box. He told the palace guards his mission and was taken to the throne room.

"Your Majesty," Chang said, "I have brought you a wonderful magic paper boat that turns into a real boat when you float it on the water." But he never said one word about Wang.

The Emperor was pleased and appointed Chang to a high office and gave him a mansion in which to live. There Chang stayed, forgetting all about Wang.

Days went by and Wang waited in his hut for Chang. He kept on cutting wood and selling it to support himself and his mother.

Often he wondered why Chang did not come back as he had promised and he wondered what had happened to his magic boat.

One day he decided to go to the capital to find out. After arranging for someone to take care of his old mother he set out, carrying some clothes and bedding in bundles on both ends of his shoulder pole. When he reached the capital he found lodging in an inn. The innkeeper told him that Chang passed by the street every morning on his way to the Emperor's court. The next day Wang waited on the street. Soon he saw Chang coming in his sedan chair, preceded by attendants carrying banners and musicians playing gongs and drums.

Wang shouted greetings to him. Chang was shocked when he saw Wang. He was frightened that Wang had come to claim his position and wealth. So he ordered the guards to drive Wang away and not to spare the use of their sticks. This they did readily, cutting Wang's face and beating all his body.

Wang limped away as best he could and lay down by the wayside, unable to walk. Then a wonderful thing happened. Some of the animals he had saved from drowning were nearby and recognized him.

A snake lying not far off sidled up to him as he lay there groaning. It was a snake with magic powers, as many animals had in those olden days. He began licking the cuts on Wang's face. At once he felt no more pain.

Then the snake glided swiftly away and returned with

a few magic healing plants in his mouth. He touched Wang's wounds with the plants and the wounds closed at once. Even the pain where he had been hit on his shoulders and legs was gone.

He rested for a time and then decided to find out why his friend had acted so meanly. As he rose, the snake said to him, "Take some of the miracle healing plants with you. You may need them someday."

Wang thanked the snake and started for the palace. When he came near the gate, he saw a crowd gathered around a proclamation on the wall, reading it. The large Chinese characters told them that the Emperor's daughter suddenly had become very ill, and the ruler promised no end of riches and even the Princess in marriage to the man who would cure her.

At once Wang thought of the miracle-curing plants the snake had given him and he asked to be taken to see the sick Princess. Soon he was in the chamber where she was lying in a curtained bed. The Emperor was there also, watching to see what Wang would do.

Wang took a miracle plant and gave it to a trusted lady-in-waiting. She rubbed the Princess from head to toe with it. At once color came back to her cheeks and lips. The lady-in-waiting kept on rubbing her with the miracle plant and soon after Wang left the Princess's room she got up and seemed all well.

Then the Emperor said, "You are a wonderful doctor, Wang, and I want you to stay in my palace. If my daughter desires it, you may marry her."

When Chang saw what had happened, he was frightened lest his treachery be discovered.

He went to the Emperor. "Your Majesty," he said, "you will let an ignorant man marry your daughter because he has a magic healing plant any other man could also have found. Why not first put him to tests to see if he is worthy of marrying a princess?"

The Emperor thought this was good advice, so he said to Chang, "You think of the proper tests to try his worthiness."

This was just what the wily fellow wanted. He went at once to the Chief Eunuch of the palace, who was his friend.

"I bring you a bar of gold, dear friend, for the many favors you have done for me. Now, once again, I will ask you to do something for me. You know the Emperor will let that peasant woodcutter marry his daughter. She is worthy of a better man, and the good Emperor has agreed to the advice I have given him. I told him to put Wang to some tests to prove himself more than a peasant. Help me think of some tasks in which he is sure to fail, for Wang is no friend of mine."

"Nor of mine," said the eunuch. "I know of one task that neither Wang nor any other man can do."

"What is it, good friend?"

"Take two measures of chaff and mix them together with two measures of fine sesame seeds and then order him to separate one from the other by the time the Sun reaches the center of the sky. No man can do that, and surely not a common woodcutter."

Chang was pleased and returned to the Emperor and told him of the test to be set to Wang to prove himself worthy of a princess. The Emperor agreed and he ordered that chaff and sesame be mixed and set in the garden pavilion. Then Wang was called.

"Wang," said the Emperor, "You are an unknown woodcutter. Before I will let you marry my daughter, you must show yourself worthy of her. Here on this bench is a chest in which two *tou** of chaff and two *tou* of sesame seeds are mixed. You must separate the sesame seeds from the chaff by the time the sun is in the middle of Heaven. That will prove you are more than just a woodcutter."

The Emperor left and Wang was alone with the sesame

* A *tou* is a measure for grain. It is made of wood and is about 316 cubic inches in volume. It is often translated as our measure, a "peck."

seeds and the chaff. No—he was not alone. In the garden insects and ants all around him were busy with their daily chores.

Now it so happened that among the ants were some who were on the magic boat with Wang. They saw how downhearted he looked.

"Why so sad?" the ants asked.

"I am sad because I was told I would have to separate the sesame seeds from the chaff by the time the sun is in the center of Heaven. No man can do that."

"True," the ants said, and they shook their jointed bodies with laughter. "True, no man can do it, but ants can. You saved our lives, and now we will help you. Just watch us."

By this time hundreds of ants had gathered around Wang.

"Come to work," shouted the ants who had spoken to Wang.

The ants set to work at once, falling over one another, pushing, jostling, busily separating the sesame seeds from the chaff, and, before you could count to ten, the work was done, and the sun was not yet in the middle of Heaven.

The sun moved slowly in its path and soon was at the very middle when Chang and the Chief Eunuch burst into the pavilion, the Emperor following slowly. They all stopped in amazement when they saw the seeds and the chaff carefully separated into two heaps. Not a single one was intermixed with the other.

"That is truly wonderful," said the Emperor.

"But not wonderful enough for a common woodcutter to marry a princess, Your Majesty," said the Chief Eunuch. "Put him to one more test, which will be the last. If he succeeds, he will be truly worthy, Your Majesty. Here is the supreme test I would suggest. Seat the Princess among fifty-three maidens, all dressed alike, all sitting in flower chairs. If he can choose the Princess from among the fifty-four, then he can marry her."

The Emperor agreed, and the trial was set for the next day. It would be held again in the royal garden.

Wang could not sleep from excitement and worry. When the first glow of dawn came into the sky, he was in the garden looking at the fifty-four "flower chairs" set out.

The garden was full of morning life:—ants, insects, birds, butterflies, and pigeons were busy hunting, and bees were zooming from flower to flower in their usual way. Some of those who had been sheltered by Wang recognized him.

"Why so sad, Master Wang?" they zoomed. "Why so sad when all around you is sunshine and warmth?"

"I am sad because soon I will be given a test that I know I will fail."

"What is that terrible test?" they zoomed merrily.

"To find which is the Princess among fifty-four maidens, all dressed alike and seated in these flower chairs you see there. How can I find her among fifty-four?"

"Easily, easily," zoomed the bees. "Easily, with our help. You helped us, now we will help you. The Princess loves bees and sweet honey. We will swarm around her flower chair. In this way you will be able to recognize her."

A door opened, and the maidens, chattering, laughing, all dressed alike, seated themselves in the flower chairs. The chairs were then borne on the shoulders of chair carriers in a procession around the garden. Chang, the Chief Eunuch, and the Emperor also came out. Wang looked at the girls, who smiled and blushed.

"Look slowly and carefully," said the Emperor, who had begun to like Wang.

Wang looked carefully from one maiden to another. Then he came to the maiden seated in the chair around which the bees were zooming merrily, as they had promised.

"That is the Princess," Wang said, as he pointed to the maiden around whom the bees were swarming merrily.

"That is the Princess," Wang shouted a second time.

"Truly," said the Emperor, "Wang, you are worthy of marrying my daughter."

And married they were and lived a happy life, and so did Wang's mother.

As for Chang, when the Emperor heard the complete story, Chang was punished properly for his misdeeds.

# THE SAD TALE OF THE RABBIT'S TAIL

HAN

漢

This happened in China in the days when animals joked and argued and played tricks on one another.

Two rabbits were hopping around merrily on the green grass beside a gentle running river.

"Look," said one of the rabbits, "just look at that green grass on the other side of the river. It looks greener and more delicate than the grass on our side."

The other rabbit looked across the river. "Yes," he said, "what you say is true, Brother Rabbit, but what good is that to us? To get at that sweet, young grass we must cross this wide river. And we cannot swim. Wishing is not getting us there." For a while both were silent.

Then the first rabbit spoke again, "I have an idea that will get us to the other side."

"What is your idea?"

"See that big, fat turtle sunning herself in the glowing

warmth? Now, listen and watch, and soon we will be on the other side."

The rabbit raised his voice and shouted, "Auntie Turtle, I was told that you said there are more turtles in your family than there are rabbits in my family, but I tell you, you are all wrong. My family is much bigger than yours, fat as you are, old as you are, and strong as you are."

"You are a braggart," gulped the turtle, "I tell you, I have more children in my family than you have in yours."

Rabbit laughed and screamed, "Bragging is silly talk. You must prove your words."

"Well, let us count our children," gurgled Turtle. "That will show who is right."

"Agreed," cried Rabbit. "Get your family together right now here on the river. I will count them. Then I will gather my family on the bank and you can count them."

"Agreed," purled Turtle, and began calling her family. They came and Turtle shouted, "Lie down, one next to the other, so that this silly, bragging rabbit can count you. Let him see that my family is bigger than his."

The turtles did as they were told. They made a line that stretched from one side of the river to the other.

Both rabbits began hopping on the shells of the turtles, counting as they skipped from one turtle to another. They finished counting when they were on the far side of the river, just where they wanted to be.

The first rabbit turned to Turtle in the river and shouted, "Hi there, you silly turtle, you are very foolish! All we wanted was to get across the river on your shell backs."

Turtle gurgled and growled in anger at having been fooled. She crawled as fast as she could on to the bank. The rabbits, proud of their trick, did not notice anything. And . . . before they knew what was happening, Turtle bit off the rabbits' tails.

And that is why, ever since then, rabbits have short, stumpy tails as a punishment for fooling other animals.

# A
# TRUE
# MONEY
# TREE

HAN

漢

In years gone by, there lived an old Chinese man by the name of Li. He had two sons, Long Life and Good Life.

Long Life's mother had died when he was a young boy, and Li had been lonely without a wife in the house. So he had married again, and when she gave him a son, he named him Good Life, for life in his house was good. But alas! the new wife did not like Long Life, so she made him do all the hard work in the house and in the fields and garden. But Long Life was an obedient son and did not complain. He did all that had to be done while his stepmother and ‚brother looked on.

When he was seventeen years old, his father died, and his life with his stepmother was made even harder than it had been before. Although he did all the work in the house and fields, he was scolded all the time. No matter how much he tried to please his stepmother, she was always finding fault with him. She was always thinking of ways to get rid of him.

So one day she said, "You are old enough to be on your own now. We should divide the land your father left. Your brother is still young, and he can stay with me. We should each live in our own home, then there will be no quarrel between us."

Long Life agreed to this and left the division of property to his stepmother. She took the house and the best fields around it for herself and her son. To Long Life she gave a barren piece of land on a hill far from the village.

Long Life did not complain. He built himself a little hut and began clearing the land and plowing and planting on it. He cut some firewood, and little by little he grew enough food to support himself nicely.

With Long Life gone from the house and land where he had done all the work, there was no one to do it. Good Life and his mother were lazy and careless, so they became poorer and poorer. One day the mother said to her son, "Look, we have a fine house and good land, and your brother lives in a hut on a piece of barren and hilly land, but he is getting richer and we are getting poorer. I am sure your father left him something of which we did not get our share. Son, go to your brother and make him tell you the truth, and ask him why he is getting rich and we are becoming poor. Tell him if he got something from his father we don't know about, he must give us at least half of it."

Good Life came to his brother in his little hut and said, "Brother, did our father give you some treasure we don't know about? We have fine land and you have a rocky barren piece—how is it that you are doing so well and we so poorly? You have plenty of everything and we have nothing. Did our father leave something you are hiding from us? We want our share of it."

"Brother, you are right. Our wise father left me a wonderful treasure—a money tree. It has two trunks and there are five branches on each trunk. All my food and clothing depend on that wonderful tree. From that tree I will always get enough money to live in good health and pleasure . . . it—"

Good Life broke in, "Where is that tree? Where are you hiding it?"

"I am not hiding it. It is with me all the time on my little piece of land, in my garden, and I am always there working at it. It gives me food, drink, and clothes and anything else I need, and if you—"

Before he could finish his words, Good Life rushed out and ran to his home. "Mother, Mother," he cried, "you were right. My father left a money tree that will give us money for all we need, but Long Life took it. He told me. It will give money for food, clothes, and everything else we need."

"I knew we were cheated," she cried. "Run to Long Life's orchard and dig up that money tree and plant it in our garden. It should be here."

Good Life did not need any coaxing. He found a spade and ran to Long Life's garden. He searched for a long time until he found a tree with two trunks and ten branches. He worked hard digging it up. Then he dragged it to his mother's garden and there he dug a deep hole and planted the tree, watering it well. Day after day he watered the tree and shook it hard—but no money fell from it.

Then Good Life went back to his brother in anger and cried, "I took a tree with two trunks and ten branches from your garden, and planted it in our garden, watered it and took care of it, but no money falls from it. Did you tell me the truth?"

"Dear brother, I told you the truth—but you did not wait to hear the end of what I had to say. My money tree can never be stolen. It is my two arms and hands. The arms are the trunks and the fingers are the branches. Use them for planting trees and crops and to do all other work. Then money will come from them, and that will get you everything you need. My arms and hands are my fortune and I call them my money tree. You have a money tree, too. Put it to work as I do, and you will have all the money you need to buy whatever you want."

Good Life went home to his mother. On the way he had been thinking of his brother's words. "Mother," he said, "now I have the true money tree and . . ." He put his hands to work and soon he and his mother reaped money from that tree for food and everything else, just as his brother did.

# THE RED STREAM

HAN

Once upon a time in old China there lived two young people, just married, who would have been very happy if not for the husband's stepmother, who lived with them. She never stopped finding fault with the youthful wife. Whatever the young bride did, it was wrong. Matters became so bad that the two young ones decided to run away.

One night, when the stepmother was in deep sleep, they took two horses from the stable and rode off.

They rode all night, and in the morning they came to a mountain. There they saw a sight they had never seen before: a sparkling stream of red water! All along the stream there were red flowers; even the grass was red!

Said the young wife Yü Hua, "I have never seen such a red stream, but I am thirsty and I will drink from it."

"Take a good drink," said Shih Tun, her husband, and she did. The two horses also drank the red water.

No sooner did Yü Hua drink the water than she felt as rested as if she had had a good night's sleep. The horses, too, seemed sprightly and refreshed.

The husband and wife rode on briskly for some time until they came to a hut with a straw-thatched roof, before which stood a kindly looking old woman.

"'Where are you riding, nice young people?" she said.

"We are just riding, good lady, to where our horses will lead us."

"Why not stay with me a little? I live alone, and it would be good to see two young ones in my home."

"Gladly," said Yü Hua.

The two got off their horses and joined the old woman, helping her around the house and preparing the food.

While they were eating the evening meal, Yü Hua told of the wonderful red water she had drunk and how it seemed to give her new strength.

The old woman turned pale when she heard this and cried, "What a pity! Why did you drink that water? The Red Stream belongs to a fierce monster. Its beginning is on the Red Mountain in the roots of a giant maple tree. When the leaves turn red in the fall, the tree becomes a monster who claims as his bride any girl who drinks from the red water. With the first snow, the monster will turn into a maple tree again, and so will the girl."

"He cannot claim my wife; I will keep her. I am not afraid of a monster," cried Shih Tun.

They stayed with the old woman, helping her in every way. Fall came. Everything was ripe and they gathered fruits and vegetables. The leaves of the maple trees turned red and began falling.

One day when the three were sitting behind the hut shelling chestnuts, the wind blew a red leaf before them. It whirled around and around and suddenly in the whirling wind there was the monster with a fierce red face. He waved the billowing sleeve of his red robe and the red leaf became a bridal flower chair. The whirlwind put Yü Hua into the bridal chair and took her up high in the air to the Red Mountain to the cave where the monster lived.

At first Shih Tun was speechless. Then he cried, "I must find Yü Hua. I will go to the Red Mountain and bring her back!" He picked up his long sharp sword, bade the old woman good-by, mounted his horse, and rode hard and fast in the direction of the Red Mountain.

In his cave in the Red Mountain, and before Yü Hua could come out of her fright, the monster had turned himself into a handsome young man.

"Yü Hua," he said, "I have brought you here to become my bride."

"Never," said Yü Hua, "Shih Tun is my husband and I love only him."

"You are in my power and you will never see Shih Tun again. You are mine."

"I am not; Shih Tun will rescue me."

Right then they heard the sound of a horse's hoofs, and the monster saw Shih Tun coming.

He took off the striped sash that was wound around his waist, spoke magic words, and the sash became a tiger who swallowed Shih Tun and his horse. Unafraid, Shih Tun slashed his way out of the beast. When his sword touched the belly of the tiger, it turned back into the sash, all tattered and torn.

When the monster saw this, he tore off from the cave wall a scroll, on which a mountain was painted, and threw it at Shih Tun. He spoke magic words and it became a real mountain.

Shih Tun got on his horse and tried to ride over the mountain, but the mountain was too steep. He got off his horse and tried to climb up. With rocks all over and the ground slippery and jagged, he kept falling. The perspiration was coming down his forehead into his eyes. He wiped it off with his hands and flung it at the stones. At once the magic left the mountain and it became a paper scroll again, hanging wet and limp on a tree branch in front of the monster's cave.

"You will never have Yü Hua," cried the monster. He brushed his sleeve over her and she instantly stood still. She could not move or utter a single word. Next he spoke magic words and waved his sleeves at two embroidered pillows near her. They were immediately turned into human figures looking exactly like Yü Hua, but they too could not move or speak. . . . The monster had disappeared.

"Yü Hua! Which one of these three is my wife? Where are you? I have overcome many hardships to reach you. Which one are you? Speak to me." The three statues were silent. Yü Hua wanted to speak, but she could not. Tears began to flow from her eyes, and Shih Tun knew at once which was Yü Hua. He took her in his arms and tried to get on his horse. But she was stiff and heavy as a stone, so he began walking, carrying the dead weight in his arms. Slowly he went over hill and dale until he came to a forest of maple trees. There he sat down to rest.

"I shall never leave you! You will always be with me, even if you have been turned into stone," he said to the still figure of Yü Hua.

At these words the monster stood before Shih Tun. Shih Tun lifted his sword to attack him.

"Hold your weapon," said the monster, tears glistening in his eyes. "A love like yours moves even someone like me, whose heart is as hard as flint. Such love should be rewarded, not destroyed. . . . Yü Hua will again be as she was, and you will be happy with her."

As he spoke he began slowly to turn into a giant maple tree.

On the maple tree's red leaves glistened silver dew drops; those were the tears of the monster. When Shih Tun carried Yü Hua past the tree, the dew drops fell on her body,

and she came to life again—she could speak and move about easily.

Shih Tun and Yü Hua walked down the Red Mountain and came to the thatched-roof hut, where the old woman welcomed them with open arms.

From then on, the three lived happily together, and from then on it was safe to drink the water of the Red Stream. As for the giant red maple tree, it never again turned into a monster.

TIBETO-
BURMAN

藏缅

# THE TALE
# OF THE
# GOLDEN VASE
# AND THE
# BRIGHT MONKEYS

TIBETAN

A merry tale, a wise tale, a witty tale.
   One that will bring you a pleasant smile as it did to ancient Tibetan folks and as it does to Chinese people everywhere.

   Once upon a time in old China there lived in Tibet two friends, Dorje and Sonam, a little distance from each other. Just the same, they often worked together on their land.

   One day they decided to go to the mountaintop to look for *jen-shen* fruits.

   They searched and dug most of the day without much success, when suddenly Dorje's spade hit something hard. Both now dug eagerly and soon they took out a vase that gleamed in the setting sun.

   "It is pure gold!" cried Sonam, brushing the earth from it.

"I am not so sure," said Dorje slyly. "I am not so sure. We must test it first."

"That's a good idea," said Sonam.

"Good," said Dorje. "I will take the vase to a friend of mine who is a goldsmith. He can tell us." But in his mind there were mean dishonest thoughts of how he could keep the golden vase for himself.

"If it is really gold, I will sell it to him and we will share the money."

Sonam, who trusted his friend, agreed, and the two friends parted, deciding to meet soon again, to divide the money if the vase was truly of gold, and then to go again to look for *jen-shen* fruits.

Dorje soon learned the vase was of gold, but he decided to keep it all for himself. So two days later, when his friend came again, he greeted him with a long, sad face.

"What is wrong, dear Dorje? You look so sad."

"Alas!" Dorje said, "I took the vase to show it to the goldsmith and accidentally put it near the fire. The vase was only cheap pewter and melted into a lump of worthless metal."

Sonam did not quite believe this, but he just said, "Never mind, we only found the vase by accident. If it is not worth anything, we have lost nothing."

Dorje was very happy that Sonam took the bad news well. He was so pleased that he asked his wife to prepare a fine meal to entertain his friend.

The next day when they were saying good-by to each other, Sonam said, "Dear friend Dorje, I want to thank you for your hospitality and all the trouble you took with the vase. In return I would like to invite your two dear children to my home. You have mountains here, but I have a pond as well as mountains, and many fruit trees. They can play with the rabbits and pigeons I keep, swim in the pond, and eat fruits to their hearts' desire. It would be a nice vacation for them. Why not send them to my home for a little time?"

The children shouted with joy when they heard this, and their father Dorje readily agreed.

Sonam held the children by the hand and started to lead them to his home. He was a kind man and loved children. He gave them sweetmeats to eat. On the way, they came to a mountain called "Monkey Hill," because many monkeys lived there.

Sonam said, "There are so many monkeys, we will catch some to play with."

The children shouted with pleasure and ran ahead of Sonam. They came to the woods where monkeys leaped from branch to branch, chattering and screaming.

The children were truly excited and ran around with the playful monkeys.

Sonam looked on for a while. Then he caught two very young animals and put them in a twig cage he had with him.

"We will play with those little fellows," Sonam said to the children. They went to his home gaily, happily shouting and running.

When they were at Sonam's home, he said, "I will give each little monkey the same name you have, and you must help me teach them each trick you know."

The young monkeys were good students, and the children and Sonam spent happy hours playing together. The young monkeys learned to imitate the children's walk and motions of their hands and head, and the children and Sonam laughed and laughed.

One day a friend of the family came to tell them that Dorje was coming the next day to take the children home. The next morning Sonam gave each of the children a large basket and said, "Go up the mountain to where the crickets are chirping in the woods. There you will find berries and all the fruits you like. Be sure to fill your baskets. Your father is coming for you and we will all have a nice feast before you go home."

When they were gone and Sonam heard Dorje coming, he sat down on the ground, holding a young monkey on each arm, and put on a long, sad face.

"What is wrong, friend?" cried Dorje.

"Woe!" moaned Sonam, "I am sorrowing for your two lovely children."

"What is wrong? What happened to them? Where are they?"

"They are here, friend Dorje. A weird thing happened to your two children. One day they suddenly turned into the little monkeys I am holding on my arms." He pulled each monkey's tail and, as they had been trained, at that signal they jumped off his arms and began to walk and dance as the children did. Then Sonam called them by the children's names and they came up just as they had been taught.

Dorje looked on, too surprised to talk. He sat silent for a few moments. Then he stuttered, "How did this happen? How could such a thing happen? How is this possible?"

"True, dear friend Dorje, it is a freak happening, but strange things happen all the time. Remember the strange affair of the golden vase turning into cheap pewter?"

For a moment Dorje seemed stunned. Then he looked at Sonam and an understanding smile came to his face.

"I understand, dear friend! Now, tell me where my children are, and I will give you half of the money I got for the gold vase. It was stupid of me to want to keep it all."

"They will soon be here, Dorje. They went to gather berries and fruits for us."

"Good," said Dorje. "That will give me time to bring half the money I owe you."

He ran and returned just as the children came with the baskets full of berries and fruits.

Everyone, even the two little monkeys, enjoyed a grand feast. And Dorje and Sonam remained understanding friends.

# THE
# BIRD OF
# HAPPINESS

TIBETAN

In the wildest and bleakest place of Tibet in China, once upon a time there was a sad village with sad people. For them, though near the sky, the golden sunshine did not shine, there were no budding trees or colorful flowers, birds did not sing, and winds did not whisper. All was cold, sad, and silent.

But the old folks, hungry and freezing, told of a Bird of Happiness that lived on a snowy mountain far away in the east who could give happiness to the village if only someone would bring it to them.

Year after year some young men, fearless and courageous, set forth to capture that bird, but none came back; for the Bird of Happiness was guarded by three monsters whom no one could overcome.

One year, after a winter of biting cold and bitter hunger, the elders asked Wang-ga, one of the young men, to undertake the heroic deed that would bring them cheer and joy.

Wang-ga was big and strong and fearless, and he set off. Day in day out he trudged up the steep mountains of Tibet, where the snow glistened like silver, toward the home of the Bird of Happiness.

Up stony paths, over boulders and fallen trees he went. Suddenly a giant monster stood before him! His wild, tangled black beard reached to his feet, his ears were long and pointed and covered with bristles; in his hairy hand he held a long spear. In a croaking voice he cried:

"Who dares to come to my home? Who are you? What do you want?"

"I have come to find the Bird of Happiness for the people of my suffering village."

The monster thundered: "You must first kill the mother of Lo-san before you can even see that Bird; otherwise you must walk on sharp pointed rocks for thirty-three stations."*

"I will not kill the mother of Lo-san. I love my mother and I love all mothers and I will never hurt any of them."

At that the monster blew wildly down his black beard and at once the ground was strewn with big jagged stones as sharp as knives, and the monster was gone.

Wang-ga began struggling over the jagged rocks. His boots and clothes were torn; his feet and hands were bleeding. But he kept on going from station to station, full of courage and hope, until he reached the thirty-third station! But there, on a steep rock covered with snow, stood yet another monster! More fierce-looking than the first, his long yellow beard was full of knots and reached to the snow. His two front teeth hung to his chin, and the nails of his fingers were long and sharp.

"Where are you going, Wang-ga?" he growled. His voice was like the roaring wind.

---

* Stations are stopover places for horses. They are called "horse stations" and are about 80 Chinese *li* apart, or almost 30 miles.

"I am going to find the Bird of Happiness and bring him to my suffering village."

"You will never get that bird unless you rid us of the old man Ssu-lang."

"Never will I harm the old man Ssu-lang. I love my own grandfather, and I will never harm anyone else's grandfather."

"Then you must travel thirty-three more stations—and without any food!"

He blew up his cheeks, let out a wild breath, and the bag with food Wang-ga carried on his shoulders blew high, high into the sky, and the monster vanished! The mountains and rivers turned into a vast desert. Nothing grew on the land. There was nothing Wang-ga could find to eat.

Fearless and hungry, Wang-ga went on and on over the endless sand. He was famished and thirsty, but the thought of finally reaching the Bird of Happiness kept him going from station to station. By the time he came to the last station, he was only skin and bones and hoped it was the end—but no, before him rose another monster! Bigger and wilder-looking than the others, his white beard was as hoary as the frost.

"Where are you going?" he roared. "You miserable bag of skin and bones!"

"I am going to get the Bird of Happiness for my suffering village."

"You will never get the Bird of Happiness unless you tear out the eyes of the beautiful maiden Pai-ma."

"Never! Never!" cried Wang-ga with the little strength left in him. "I will never tear out Pai-ma's beautiful eyes, or anyone else's eyes."

"Then, out with your eyes!" The monster took a deep breath, blowing up his cheeks like sails, and then he let out a fierce breath in Wang-ga's face, and it took the eyes out of Wang-ga's head, and he was blind!

"Now you must travel thirty-three stations over rocks and trees, blind as you are!" And the monster was gone!

Blind! Hands outstretched, Wang-ga stumbled and

groped along slowly. Station after station! Station after station! It was body- and heartbreaking, but he kept on with hope and courage. His hands were bleeding, his feet were bleeding, but he went on.

He knew he was going higher and higher, for it was growing colder and he felt the hard-packed snow under his feet. He knew he was getting near the Bird of Happiness.

Suddenly he heard the sound of wings!

"You must be the bird that will bring us happiness!" he cried.

"I will help you, but first I must give you back your eyes!"

The Bird of Happiness stroked Wang-ga's eyelids gently with its fluttering wings, and lo! Wang-ga saw the sun and the mountains once again. The wounds on his body healed and flesh returned to his body.

The Bird of Happiness gave him meat and butter-cakes to eat. Wang-ga cried joyfully, "Heavenly Bird of Happiness! I have come to beg you to come to my village, which is cold and dreary. You can give us what we want most in life—happy living!"

The bird replied: "I will gladly come with you to bring joy to all. Now, get on my wings and we will fly to your village."

Wang-ga got on the wide wings of the beautiful Bird of Happiness and, before he knew it, they were in the village.

Then the bird began to sing. It was a beautiful song and, as he was singing, slowly the golden sun appeared over the village, bringing warmth to everything. The birds sang again, and trees sprang up over the hills that were bare, and their branches began showing leaves and blossoms. Wild flowers of every color grew all over the earth. The Bird of Happiness kept on singing, and green fields appeared with a shining broad river winding through them. There was joy everywhere, and from then on the village was truly happy, and so were its people.

# THE
# TIBETAN
# ENVOY'S
# MISSION

TIBETAN

This is a tale of wonders that Tibetan folk, living in Szechuan, tell of bygone days. Then life was different, but people were the same as they are today.

Listen!

Once there lived in the Chinese capital the great emperor of the T'ang dynasty with the title of T'ai-tsung, who had a beautiful daughter called Wen-ch'eng, whom many wanted to marry. Nobles and kings sent their envoys to the capital Ch'ang-an to ask for her hand. Once seven kings sent their envoys to propose at the same time. One of them was from the ruler of Tibet. The men were received with great honors, even the envoy from Tibet, though the Emperor hoped he would never have to marry his daughter to a man who lived so far away. To avoid offending anyone, the Emperor asked his wise ministers to make up difficult tests as a condition of marriage, tests in which all the envoys would have a chance to compete.

The ministers held a council and decided on tasks they were sure no one could fulfill. He who could carry them out would have the Princess for his master. The envoys agreed, and the days for the trials were set.

When the envoys arrived at the appointed place, the chief minister spoke: "In the courtyard stand five hundred of the royal horses, all mares, and their five hundred colts and fillies. The Emperor asks you to bring each young horse to its right mother."

All the envoys went into the courtyard, and there were the beautiful horses and their prancing young ones. Every envoy—except one—tried to bring each young horse to its mother, but the horses kicked wildly and the colts and fillies pranced merrily. The envoy of the Tibetan king stood aside, watching. He knew horses well, for in Tibet horses are part of a family. Then he said to the minister, "I will do it, but first the mares must be fed. After that I will bring mothers and young ones together."

The horses were then fed and so they began neighing for their young ones to come to nurse at their teats. Soon each young horse found its own mother.

But when the Emperor heard that the Tibetan envoy had won, he cried, "Set another task in which even the Tibetan will fail. I do not want my daughter to be so far away."

The chief minister was ready and he called the envoys together.

"There is another test you must solve before you can take the Princess with you. Here is a piece of glistening green jade carved with the most intricate designs. It has birds and beasts, and through them all, in this most intricate design, is a tiny tunnel twisting and turning in a hundred directions. Here is a string of silk. You must thread it through that tunnel in the jade."

One envoy after another tried and failed. Now it was

the Tibetan envoy's turn. Smilingly he thought to himself, "I must find an ant and I need a little honey."

He went into the garden and found a strong black ant and brought it in. He took the silken string and tied it to the black ant. Then he put the ant into the opening of the tunnel. The honey he smeared at the end of the tunnel. Ants love honey, and the one with the string smelled it quickly. Hurriedly it began crawling through all the winding openings to reach the honey. At last it came through the tunnel with the string still tied to it. The Tibetan envoy made a knot tying the two ends of the string together and showed the jade to the minister.

When the Emperor heard about this, he said to his minister, "Find some test the Tibetan cannot solve."

"I will, Your Majesty. I will give him the test of the tree."

He took a tree trunk and had it polished smoothly so that both ends were exactly the same dimension and brought it to the envoys.

"Which end is from the top of the tree and which is from the bottom?" he asked. One envoy after another examined the tree trunk carefully, smelled the wood, touched it, and measured it, but none could tell.

Now, Tibetans live in the mountains and know much about trees. The Tibetan envoy knew that the top of a tree is less dense and therefore lighter, while the bottom is thicker and therefore heavier. He ordered the trunk to be thrown into the water. The lighter upper part floated above the water, while the lower, heavier part lay deeper in the water, dragging behind.

The Tibetan envoy gave the minister the right answer.

When the Emperor heard this he cried, "Give him one more test. If he gets it right, I must let my daughter go to that far land."

"I will try once more," said the minister. "Let us take three hundred young court girls, the Princess among them, dress them all alike, and see if he can guess which one is the Princess."

The day was set for the final test and the envoys were told to be ready. Everyone waited except the Tibetan. He was busy going among those working in the royal palace and asking what the Princess looked like. No one knew, for the Princess was rarely seen. But in the evening he luckily found an old woman who washed the Princess's clothes. She was wise with the wisdom of years.

"I will tell you how you will know the Princess, but you must swear not to tell anyone I told you." The Tibetan envoy swore readily.

"Young noble, don't pick the prettiest. Princesses are no more beautiful than other young girls.

"Don't pick the one at the beginning or at the end of the line. The Emperor would not put his daughter where she could be found easily. And now I will tell you how you will know her. She uses a sweet-smelling lotion sent to her from a faraway land. Only she uses it. She loves its fragrance, and so do the bees and butterflies. Look for a maiden around whose head bees and butterflies buzz and flutter."

The Tibetan envoy thanked her. Then came the day when all the envoys stood before three hundred maidens, but none could guess who the Princess was. The Tibetan envoy also looked and soon saw one lovely maiden around whose head a golden bee was buzzing.

"That is the Princess," he said, pointing to her.

When the Emperor heard this, he decided that Heaven had decreed whom his daughter should marry, and so he sent her to wed the faraway King of Tibet.

# BIG BROTHER-MAN; LITTLE BROTHER-RABBIT

CH'IANG

Long, long ago, so long that even the oldest grandfathers speak of it as long, long ago, men and animals often lived together and helped one another.

At that time there lived in Szechuan Province in China a mother and a son who were very poor. They planted peas and yams, but every day a big rabbit came to their garden and ate the young fresh vegetables. He left telltale pods and skins behind a big rock.

"We must do something to stop that big rabbit from robbing us of our food," said the son.

"Son, I will tell you what to do to get rid of that thief," said the mother. "Make good, sticky pine pitch and smear it on the rock in our garden. When that rabbit comes to steal our peas and yams he will get stuck in the pitch and we will make a good stew of him."

The son did what his mother told him to do, and soon the rabbit was stuck on the rock.

When the mother saw this, she said to her son, "Fill our big kettle with water and put it on the fire, and we will cook the big rabbit."

Rabbit heard and saw and he begged, "Mother, don't cook me. I want to be your son, too, and then I can help Big Brother get food for us."

Even though mother and son knew that animals spoke in those days, they were surprised to hear Rabbit's words.

The son's heart softened and he said, "Mother, let us spare Rabbit; I am sure he will help us."

The mother agreed, so they took Rabbit off the rock and took him into the house. There the three lived happily together.

One day Rabbit said to them, "I heard that the rich man living not far from us is giving his daughter in marriage to a rich young man. Everyone has been invited, but they did not invite us! We should share some of the fine food they will have. Come, I will show you how we will get it."

Rabbit ran out on the road and Big Brother followed him. They came to a crossing and Rabbit stopped and sat down. So did Big Brother. Rabbit closed his eyes and made believe he was sleeping.

Soon the grand wedding party came along the road. In front rode the bride with her attendants and escorts, all on fine horses. Next followed many young women carrying baskets of sweets and goodies and buns and white-flour dumplings.

They saw the beautiful rabbit sleeping on a rock, hardly moving a hair. They all got off their horses and tried to catch Rabbit. But before they could hold him down, he jumped up and ran off. Everyone started to chase him. The girls bearing the buns and dumplings set the food on the ground and joined in the chase. They almost had Rabbit surrounded, but he ran away again. Back and forth he led them, farther and farther away from the food.

Big Brother was now alone with the baskets. He took as many dumplings and buns as he could carry and went home. Soon Rabbit came back and they all had a grand feast. While they were enjoying the food, Rabbit said, "Tomorrow, Mother and Big Brother, tomorrow you will have fine new clothes."

"How?" asked Big Brother. "We have no money to buy them."

"I will show you how we will get them without money! Money will come to us."

The next morning Rabbit and Big Brother started off on the road. When they came to a crossing, Rabbit said, "You wait in the forest; I will stay here."

Soon along came an official of high rank on horseback, with his followers holding aloft banners and carrying canopies to the sound of gongs and trumpets. After them were many bearers who carried chests of fine clothes and silver and gold on the ends of their shoulder poles.

Rabbit hid among the rocks until the official came near. Then he lay on a rock by the side of the road and pretended to be asleep. When the bearers of the chests saw the fat rabbit, they said, "This would make a tasty dish to go with good wine!" They set down their shoulder poles and chests and tried to catch Rabbit, but he hopped away. Back and forth he zigzagged in circles and led them all after him.

Big Brother was now alone with the chests. He took the clothes they needed and some silver and gold and went home. Soon Rabbit came home to join Big Brother and Mother.

Now the old mother had fine clothes and they had money for food. They were all very happy and time went on. . . .

One day Rabbit said to Big Brother, "Big Brother, you need a bride for your home. I will get you one and she will be beautiful!"

Big Brother was pleased, and his mother said, "Fine!"

"How will you get me a bride?" Big Brother asked.

"Leave that to me," said Rabbit, smiling and showing all his teeth.

The next morning Rabbit said, "Come with me, Big Brother, let us get on our horses." This they did and rode until they came to a large village, where they stopped before the chieftain's house. He came out and, seeing the two well-dressed travelers on fine horses, thought them important people, so he offered them friendly hospitality and invited them to come in.

Food was set before them, and the chieftain noted their silken handkerchiefs and how they gave gold and silver freely to those who served them.

"Only the rich and people of note are like that," the chieftain thought.

The next day he said to Rabbit, "I have a beautiful young daughter and she is not married."

"Why not marry her to Big Brother?" Rabbit said.

"I will gladly do that," said the chieftain.

Big Brother married the lovely girl and was very happy. But when it came time to take the young wife home, he was very worried and said to Rabbit, "How can I bring the daughter of this great chieftain to my poor home?"

"Do not worry, Big Brother, I will take care of that. I will go ahead and make the proper preparations. You wait here seven more days and then set out for home."

Rabbit sauntered on and on, taking his sweet time. On the sixth day, he suddenly remembered that the chieftain would soon send a big wedding party out. He was in a panic! But he remembered that there was another village nearby ruled by a chieftain who was harsh and cruel to those who lived under him.

So Rabbit went to him, and as luck would have it, a wild storm came up right then. The sky became black as pitch, and a howling wind screeched through the air.

Rabbit ran into the chieftain's house and cried, "Flee! Run! I am your Earth God sent from above. I warn you,

Heaven will punish you for the evil you have done to your people!" Thunder and lightning without end came with the words and the evil chieftain was terrified. He ran out of his house, shouting to his family to follow him.

The storm stopped, the evil chieftain was gone, and Rabbit came out of the house, where many of the villagers had gathered.

"Friends," Rabbit said, "your evil chieftain has been driven away by Heaven. A new one will come soon who will be just and kind. Welcome him warmly."

The people were glad to hear this, and when Big Brother arrived with his bride, he was welcomed with joy.

They celebrated and feasted for seven days and seven nights, and Rabbit brought Big Brother's mother there to live with them. Their happiness was complete.

Big Brother was a good and just chieftain, and the village and its people bloomed like spring flowers. Rabbit was happy too, but one day said,

"I have done all I could for you for sparing my life. Now you will be happy without me and I can go back to my green home."

He ran into the woods and was never seen again by Big Brother or his Mother.

# A
# WELL-
# DESERVED
# PUNISHMENT

In the grand old days when birds and beasts could talk and understood one another, Rock Pigeon and Rooster were good friends and often together. One day they had been playing for some time, and when they got tired they sat down to rest. Both were very thirsty.

"By the clouds in Heaven," crowed Rooster, "I am thirsty enough to drink a rushing river."

"So am I," cooed Rock Pigeon. "Come, friend Rooster, let us look for water."

They got up and began looking everywhere for some nice bubbling water. But, with all the looking, they could not find any well or river.

Said Rock Pigeon, "Rooster, I'll tell you what, let us dig a water hole; then we will have all the water we want."

"That is a fine idea," said Rooster.

"This looks like a good place," said Rock Pigeon, and

he set to work scratching and digging.

Now, Rooster was a lazy fellow. He thought he did enough by crowing and flapping his wings. So he just crowed and flapped his wings while Rock Pigeon scratched and dug.

Rock Pigeon worked and worked while Rooster continued to wiggle his red jagged comb, crow loudly, and flap his big wings.

"Don't you think you would do better by helping me with the digging than by crowing and flapping?" coo-cooed Rock Pigeon, who was quite angry by then.

"I am doing the best I can," said Rooster.

Rock Pigeon kept on working, for she was very thirsty, while Rooster just kept on making noises.

Suddenly there was a pleasant bubbling sound from the hole that Rock Pigeon had been digging. It was cold, refreshing water!

Rock Pigeon put her beak into the water and drank and drank until her thirst was satisfied.

"Come," crowed Rooster, "I am thirsty too," and he rushed up to the water hole in which Rock Pigeon stood.

"You did not rush to help me when I was working and digging—you never lifted a foot or beak to help! Even kind Heaven would think that is not right. I would not be surprised if Heaven would send a punishment down upon you for being so lazy. I am sure a thunderbolt will come from the sky to punish you and teach you not to be so lazy! Standing and flapping your wings and watching your friend work for you! Look up to the sky and see if a thunderbolt is coming down to punish you for being lazy, standing by and letting your best friend work for you instead of helping."

Rock Pigeon looked up as if really expecting a thunderbolt to come down to punish Rooster. Rooster was frightened and looked up to Heaven too. And ever since, every time he takes a drink, the rooster looks to Heaven to see if a thunderbolt is there to come down on him for his laziness and for not helping a friend.

# WHEN ROCKS ROLLED CRACKLING WISDOM

YI

This is a tale told in China by the Yi people thousands of years ago (and still told today), when stones spoke like men, and maybe flowers and trees and beasts did too.

In those golden days there were two brothers who lived together in the same house. Their old parents died, and, as was the custom then, Elder Brother became the head of the family.

He was mean and stingy and made the life of Younger Brother an unending misery. Finally Younger Brother could no longer bear it and so he left home. He went into the woods, built himself a hut among the trees and became a woodcutter. It was hard work and he earned very little, but he lived in peace.

One day he cut a big load of wood and, tying it with a stout rope, loaded it on his shoulders and turned homeward.

The load was very heavy and soon he was looking for a spot to rest. He had come to a big round boulder rising a little from the earth. The top of it was full of cuts and crevices, and, if you looked long enough, the upper part seemed shaped like a face, with eyes, a nose, and a broad mouth. Along the sides and all around were many crevices that looked like lines in the face of a man many years old.

Younger Brother walked slowly up the stone, threw down his load of wood, and sat down in one of the crevices. His seat was comfortable, and soft breezes fanned him on all sides. Soon he dozed off to the music of the gentle winds. Suddenly he was awakened by a hard crackling voice; it was the voice of Talking Stone, on which he was sitting.

"Hey, you!" the rocky voice spoke, "Young man, you have been sitting on my head with your heavy load of wood for a long time. You don't know how heavy you and your wood are. You might think of me a little."

"I was so full of thinking of my troubles that I didn't think of others," apologized the woodcutter. "Cutting wood, dragging it home, and having to take it to market for someone to buy is no pleasure. It is a hard life. I don't earn enough for bread and rice . . . all thanks to my older brother."

"What do you mean? Don't you have a good home in which you live happily?"

"I did, but my parents died and my older brother made my life so miserable that I had to leave. My brother kept everything our father left us and now I am very poor. Woodcutting brings little for food."

"I feel sorry for you, and your brother will be punished for his misdeeds. So I will help you," Talking Stone said. "Do you see the wide opening right below where you are sitting? That is my mouth. Put your hand in it and take out a fistful of dust you will find there. It is pure gold and with it you can buy all the things you need: food, clothes, animals . . . anything you want."

Younger Brother got up quickly, went to the crevice

that Talking Stone said was his mouth, put in his hand, took out a fistful of gold dust, and put it into his bag.

He thanked kind Talking Stone over and over again. Then he put the load of wood on his back and went to his hut. The load seemed much lighter; he was thinking of what the gold dust would buy.

He quickly made use of it. He bought clothes, tools, and animals, and fixed his home.

As time went on, Elder Brother noticed with great surprise Younger Brother's good fortune. Where did he get the money to buy all these things? Surely not from woodcutting!

He went to Younger Brother, all smiles and friendly, telling him how lucky he was to have earned so much money to buy all those fine things.

Younger Brother was trusting, so he told his older brother what had happened with Talking Stone, who had given him the gold dust from his mouth.

Elder Brother thanked him and went home.

He put on torn old clothes, worn-down shoes and a tattered turban. Dressed now in rags, he went to Talking Stone. Making a long, sad face, he sat down on the rock, moaning and groaning.

Talking Stone crackled, "You took plenty of gold dust the last time. It should have been enough. Why are you still so sad?"

"That was a different man," answered Elder Brother. "However, I am just like him. My brother was mean to me, and I cut wood for a living. I don't earn enough even to feed my family."

Talking Stone knew the man was just pretending to be poor and that he was not telling the truth; all he was after was the gold dust. But Talking Stone did not let on. Instead he said, "I am sorry to hear you are in such trouble, but I can help you. Put your hand into the large crevice that is my mouth and take out a fistful of dust you will find there. It is gold dust and will be enough to help you."

Elder Brother, who had been looking greedily at the opening the whole time, quickly put both hands into the wide opening of the rock in order to gather as much of the gold dust as he could. . . . Then he tried to pull his hands out. . . .

Talking Stone had closed the stone lips of his mouth, holding the hands tight. Elder Brother pulled and pulled, his forehead wet with sweat, but his hands were firmly caught.

He begged and cried, but Talking Stone's face smiled and he mumbled through his tight stone lips, "This will be your reward for robbing your younger brother. It will teach you not to be so greedy."

"I will never do it again. Please! Please! Please let my hands go!"

"I will hold them until you learn to be generous."

When Elder Brother did not come home, his wife came to look for him. She tried to pull out his hands, but Talking Stone held his lips tight, and all their pleading was of no use. Talking Stone sputtered and crackled that he would let the hands go only when Elder Brother learned his lesson to be kind and fair.

Day after day, Elder Brother's wife came and fed him until she had no more food. Then she came to him empty-handed and stood about helplessly. Her husband scolded, "You good-for-nothing heartless woman! Why don't you bring me some food?" His wife answered, "There is no more food and no more money. If you are hungry, I can only nurse you as I would a baby." As he was starving, he stretched his neck to take a deep draft.

When Talking Stone saw this comical sight, he burst out laughing and opened his mouth. Elder Brother suddenly felt his hands free! He pulled them out quickly, forgetting the gold dust! And ran away as quickly as he could.

He never forgot the lesson he had learned from Talking Stone and never again did he dare be so greedy and mean.

# THE WINDING- HORN VILLAGE

PAI

Once upon a time, in the beautiful land of the Pai people in China's Yunnan Province, there lived a Pai king who had a fine son and two lovely daughters. He named his son Pai Lin (White Forest), the eldest daughter Pai Hao (White Crane), and the youngest daughter Pai Kuei (White Jade).

The king's life would have been as lovely as flower-perfumed sunny days if only his son and daughters had found the right kind of wife and husbands to make their lives complete. But alas, they could not!

No daughter of any noble or neighboring king pleased the prince. In the end he asked the old and wise men of his land for help.

"If you cannot find a wife among the princesses or among the daughters of the nobles, seek one among the common people."

75

So the Pai king gave his son permission to post a proc-lamation on the door of any commoner whose daughter pleased him, and the proclamation would make the daughter of that house his bride. But this only frightened the young girls, and they hid themselves. White Forest did not know what to do, so in anger he put the proclamation on a big rock and walked off. Strangely enough, the rock rolled after him into the palace. The Pai king was so frightened he shot an arrow at the rock. It went into the stone, which rolled down to the foot of the Blue Mountain. From that day folks called the rock "Beauty Rock." But the prince was so discouraged that he left the palace and went to live among the common people.

As for his sisters . . . I will tell you about them one at a time. The older sister, White Crane, loved horses and hunting so much that she never thought of marriage.

But White Jade was different. She felt lonely and dreamed of a home with children around her. She spent her days with winging birds and creatures of the field and streams, most of all with water buffaloes. Their quiet, gentle ways suited her dreamy moods. She had her own favorite water buffalo and even learned to understand his language. And she knew he understood her. To him she confided her dreams and hopes of finding a husband. One day she said to him, "You, my faithful friend, can you lead me to where I will find the man who will make me happy all my days?"

The faithful creature nodded his head three times and the princess was very happy.

That night she got on her friendly beast and he trotted her to a beautiful village by Lake Erh Hai. The moon was shining on the water with splashing silver light, and from afar came the sweet sounds of a singing flute. White Jade was en-chanted by the music and rode about on the buffalo as if in a dream. But suddenly she was jolted awake by the call of her lady-in-waiting and found herself back at the palace gate. She spent the night in warm rest and silver-sweet dreams.

The next day she arose, washed and dressed, and went straight to her father the king.

"Dear Father," she said, "I dreamed a beautiful dream this night, and I have decided what I shall do. I have decided to marry a man whom Heaven will give me."

"Daughter, what do you mean by marrying a man Heaven will give you?"

"I will tell you how I shall find a man whom Heaven will give me: I will mount my favorite water buffalo backwards, and whatever house he will bring me to will be my home, and the son of the house will be my husband, be he rich and noble or poor and of the common people."

"That is a strange idea and unfit for the daughter of a king," her father argued with her, but it did him no good. White Jade had made up her mind and neither her father nor her friends could change it. She found her favorite water buffalo, mounted him backwards, and rode out of the palace in a pale dreamy mood.

The buffalo ambled along pleasantly for some time and in the end entered a lovely village lined with green-leaved willows and surrounded by blue mountains in a silver mist. Turning his horns this way and that way, the buffalo kept on trundling through the winding alleys and twisting paths and came to a stone house, the roof of which was thatched with golden-colored straw. Around the house lay golden-yellow pumpkins, and all over the walls hung golden-yellow dried corn.

The buffalo stopped at the door of the stone house, and the princess got off and went inside. There sat a smiling old lady, poorly dressed and weaving at her loom. The old lady could tell by White Jade's clothes and manners that she was a high-born visitor. She quickly pulled out a wooden bench and invited the princess to sit down. Then she lighted a fire to boil some water to make tea. By the flickering light of the flame she could see that her guest had a kind and gentle face and was easy to love. White Jade asked how many lived in the house and, finding that the old woman had a son, she told her unusual story while drinking her tea. In the end she asked the kind old woman if she could stay with her.

"You can stay with me as long as you wish. My son is away the whole long day working in the woods. I think you will like him; he is a very good son to me and an honest worker. Soon he will be home." And soon he stood at the door, ax in hand, a tall, handsome young man.

White Jade liked him as soon as she saw him. The young man could not take his eyes off the lovely princess. She put aside her fine cloak and immediately set to work cleaning the house, washing the clothes, and cooking and serving the food as good daughters-in-law did in those days.

The young man and the princess soon were married, and one day White Jade went back to the palace to ask her father to visit her and meet her husband. Black clouds of anger came over the face of the king. He replied, "I shall never come to visit you unless you pave the road to the palace with silver inlaid with gold bricks, and build a bridge of gold to cross the river."

One day the old woman became ill and money was needed to pay for a doctor. At once the princess took off one of her golden bracelets from her arm.

"Take it, dear husband," she said. "Sell it and we will have the money for the doctor."

Her husband took it and looked at it. "What is this yellow metal you have given me?"

"That is gold, and the merchants will pay well for it."

"That is funny," he replied. "In the forest where I cut wood there is much of this yellow metal, and also white metal. I did not know that it was worth anything."

The next day he did not cut much wood, so that he could carry home a heavy rock of yellow metal he found.

When White Jade saw it, she laughed and said, "This is gold, and it will give us enough money so we can live like the nobles at my father's court."

The doctor came, was paid, and soon the kind old woman was in good health again.

From then on, the woodcutter cut little wood, but brought home gold and silver instead.

One day White Jade said to her husband, "I would like to see my father again and ask him to come here, but he said he would not come unless I paved the road to the palace with silver inlaid with gold bricks and built a bridge of gold over the river."

"That is easy for me, good wife," and he set to work at once paving the road with silver inlaid with gold bricks and building a bridge of gold over the river. When he was done, there were even some gold bricks left to present to the king as a gift.

White Jade went to the king and told him what her husband had done. At that, the king was greatly pleased. He set off at once, stepping over each gold brick on the road. His eyes were dazzled by the golden bridge with its golden balustrades and golden carved lions and phoenixes. With his officials and generals, he soon arrived at his daughter's humble home.

There he met his son-in-law and his mother and called them his new relatives, saying, "From now on your son is a prince of my land."

To this day, when the sun shines on the road to the Winding-Horn Village, the stones of the pavement shimmer and gleam like silver and gold!

# T'IEN
# THE BRAVE,
# HERO OF THE
# HSIA RIVER

T'UCHIA

People of every land in the world have their heroes. Big men, brave men, men who carry out justice, men who help those who need help. China has such heroes, and the greatest of all among the T'uchia people of Hunan Province was T'ien the Brave. He was a giant in size and strength, protecting the weak and battling for justice. Many, many tales are told of his famous deeds, but the most famous of all is his last on the Hsia River.

About a hundred *li* from T'ien's home flowed the big, broad Hsia River. Boats were always going up and down that river, carrying people, grain, fruits, and goods to other parts of Hunan.

There by the river was a large wharf for loading and unloading. Near the wharf there was an inn for stopping over. But boatmen and travelers kept away from that inn as from poison snakes. It had an ugly nickname, "The Black Inn," because guests were often robbed there—and even murdered! Folks kept away from that inn.

One time T'ien and a few of his friends were floating logs down the Hsia River and as night came they were near the big wharf and the Black Inn. T'ien said they would land there for the night. His companions begged him to go on, warning him of the danger. But T'ien laughed at them and said, "Danger is my daily pleasure. To the Black Inn we will go, and I will teach those robbers how to behave decently."

They stopped at the wharf and went into the Black Inn, where they were welcomed by the innkeeper and a number of his men.

When night came, the travelers lay down to sleep. But T'ien lay there with eyes open. When the moon hid behind the clouds, the innkeeper and some of his henchmen took away his raft and pounced on T'ien and his companions to rob them and kill them. It was just what T'ien was waiting for.

He leaped up with a great shout, picked up the innkeeper and his men like a bundle of straw and threw them into the sky. It took them a long time to drop back to earth.

Never before had that gang of robbers been treated like that. They were all frightened to death and decided to stay away from the inn until that giant of strength was gone.

But they made a mistake. T'ien liked the inn and decided to stay and make it a safe place. He asked the passing rafts to bring him some big rocks, and with these he made the wharf strong and secure against the swift current. All the travelers were happy to stay in T'ien's inn.

The innkeeper, who had grown rich there by robbing and stealing, was furious. "I must drive that monster from here," he kept on saying to his fellow thieves.

Near the wharf lived some men as dishonest as himself. He went to them and said, "A fellow has robbed me of my inn. Help me to kill him and I will pay you well for it." They quickly agreed and went to the inn at once. It was late in the afternoon and T'ien was sitting on the wharf tying his logs together. T'ien knew why they had come.

Not knowing T'ien, they asked him where T'ien was.

I told you, T'ien knew full well why they had come. So he said:

"Oh, T'ien, I know him well. He is my teacher, and he is a good teacher. I will call him for you. Watch!"

He ran to his boat and began climbing up the mast faster than a monkey.

"Teacher! Teacher!" he cried, "Come here. Some visitors have come to see you!" Then he began swinging with his big hands around and around the mast like a wheel. Next he jumped down and began twisting the heavy logs as if they were peacock feathers.

The men looked on, open-eyed and stone-frozen. They were held silent by an iron hand of fear. Finally one whispered, "If the pupil is so strong and agile, what must the teacher be like. We will not wait! Let us run off before he comes!" Off they went and told the innkeeper to keep his gold.

But the innkeeper was not ready to give up hope to regain his lair. He would try again. He had heard of a big powerful giant. Folks said he was a great fighter, so the innkeeper went to him. He stood before a towering man, a master of *kungfu*.

"Friend," he said to the fighter, "friend, a fellow robbed me of my inn. Get rid of him for me and I will pay you any amount of gold you ask."

The fighter readily agreed and set out at once.

T'ien saw him coming to the wharf and quickly guessed the reason. He was standing at the entrance to the inn and invited the fellow to come in.

"Are you looking for T'ien?" he asked, innocent-like.

"Yes, I want to see him," the fighter said.

"I know him well. I am one of his pupils. Come inside, you can wait for him over a cup of tea." The young giant went in and T'ien brewed him some tea. Then he said, "Here is a pipe and you can have a little smoke."

There were some brass rods standing near the charcoal stove. T'ien took up one of the rods and began turning and squeezing it in his hands. Soon he had squeezed the rod into powder!

"I'll put this powdered brass into a pipe for you, then you can smoke just as T'ien does. My good teacher and all his pupils smoke brass powder instead of tobacco. Here, take it and see if you like it."

The young fellow became scared white. He had never seen any man turn a brass rod into powder with his hands and use it for tobacco. He rose quickly and walked to the door.

"I'll come back another time to see your teacher. I won't wait now." And without another word he ran out.

But the innkeeper kept on in his vicious attempts, and in the end, alas, he succeeded in murdering T'ien by stealth. When T'ien was breathing his last breath, he called his wife and said to her:

"Wife, you must avenge my death. Take me and the mattress on which I am lying to the Hsia River and there shout my name three times to Heaven. Each time you cry my name, bite into the mattress. When you have cried and bitten three times, throw me and the mattress into the Hsia River and then run as fast as you can to the highest top of the hill."

The wife did exactly what T'ien told her to do.

She took the mattress and her husband to the Hsia River. There she called his name three times and bit into the mattress three times. On the third shout, she threw T'ien and the mattress into the river. Then she ran swiftly up the hill. The Hsia River began rising rapidly. It crossed the wharf and it covered the inn, drowning all the robbers in it.

From then on there has been peace on the Hsia River. And from then on the T'uchia people who live near the Hsia River have thought of T'ien the Brave as the hero who always came to their aid whenever they were in need of it.

# WHY THE SUN RISES WHEN THE ROOSTER CROWS

HANI

In very ancient days the Hani people were not a happy people. They were plagued by the glare and heat of nine giant suns that were always shining and burning, and they did not know how to get rid of them.

They had endless meetings, with oceans of words, but still they had no idea how to rid themselves of the glare and heat of nine suns. Their lives were miserable. Nothing grew in the earth; they were hungry.

Each day they met and discussed different ideas on how to get rid of so many suns. One day one of the elders said, "The best thing would be to make a giant winnowing basket and shield the suns in the sky with it."

"Good, but how will we tie the winnowing basket to the sky?" And so like many of their plans, the idea was not carried out.

The glare and the heat became worse.

One day another of the elders cried, "Let us stay in caves under the earth where the heat will not reach us."

"Then who will plant and reap? We will starve to death!"

Plan after plan was proposed but not a single one could be used.

Finally one of the oldest among the elders said, "Why not beg Urpupolo, the great bushy giant, to help us? He is the strongest man in our land and his weapons are the deadliest in all the world. Let us go to him and beg him to shoot the suns with his powerful arrows."

"Yes, only Urpupolo can help us. We must ask him!" came the cry from all sides.

So a man was chosen to go to Urpupolo, who lived in a deep dark cave. There he sat silently. He was a giant in size, with wild hair all over his head, bushy as a mound of hay. His eyebrows were coal black and hung over his gleaming eyes, and his waist was as thick as a great tree trunk.

The messenger stood before him and spoke. "Urpupolo, great giant of our land, I have come to you to ask you to help us, unless you want to see all the Hani people die."

"Who is threatening you?" grumbled Urpupolo in a deep voice.

"Great giant Urpupolo," continued the man, "nine suns sit in the sky trying to destroy us with their fierce glare and heat. We cannot plant, and many of us are going blind. Only you can help us. Destroy eight of the suns with your powerful arrows. One sun will be enough for us. We will then have a happy life."

"That is easy and I will help you."

He lifted his huge body off the ground and picked up his big bow and arrow. Then he took a few giant steps and stood in the middle of the land. The nine suns were over him in the sky, shining fiercely. He put one of the arrows on his bow, took careful aim at a sun and . . . twang! it fell with a thundering hissing noise into the black water.

Urpupolo shot seven more arrows and each hit its mark. Sun after sun fell, and each one sank deep, deep into the endless dark water.

The ninth sun, seeing how all his brothers were destroyed, was seized with fear and fled behind a giant mountain so swiftly that Urpupolo did not see him.

Now the whole world was dark and cold, but Urpupolo found his way home to his cave. But the Hani people did not like the darkness. They liked light—not burning, but warm, good light. Soon they were as unhappy as they had been before. It was dark and cold . . . no plants, no growth!

"The sun must come out from behind the mountain," the elders cried, and so did all the Hani people.

They shouted in the direction of the mountain, begging the sun to come out. But the ninth sun felt safe behind the big mountain and stayed there.

Again meetings were held. Everyone, old and young, argued about how the sun could be coaxed to come from behind the mountain.

"We must use sweet and begging voices!"

"But we all did beg with our sweetest voices."

"It must be a voice sweeter than ours," one of the elders said.

"Why not ask a bird?"

This seemed like a good idea and many birds were named. In the end they agreed on the golden oriole.

The golden oriole was proud of her voice and happy she was chosen. She flew high in the air in front of the mountain, singing proudly in the most enchanting tones for the sun to come out, for the birds wanted the sun as much as the Hani people did. But with all the pleading songs, the sun would not come from behind the mountain. Maybe Urpupolo was still there with his arrows!

The Hani people were in despair.

"Let us try another bird," someone suggested, and the choice fell on the skylark.

The skylark was proud of his voice and happy to be chosen. He was sure he could bring back the sun.

The bird flew high, high up in the blue air and began his sweet song, begging the sun to come out. He sang a long time, but it was of no use. No sun came out from behind the mountain.

The Hani people were in hopeless misery.

"We must try again; we must not give up. There must be some bird who can coax the sun out."

"Let us try the thrush! He has a sweet pleading voice. Perhaps he will succeed," another cried. The others agreed.

So they asked the thrush. He was a proud bird who thought he had the finest of all voices.

"Just let the sun hear me," he cried, "and he will surely come out." He raised his voice and warbled and trilled with all his might. But though he tried again and again, the sun would not come out.

The Hani people were in black distress.

"We must get the sun to shine on us and our land. We must, or we will all die!"

Everyone was thinking and thinking. Then one of the younger men spoke, "We have asked birds of high degree to plead for the sun to come from behind the mountain. Let us try some bird not so famous. Maybe he can plead better."

"We will try any bird! Name him!" came from all.

"Let us give the beautiful rooster a chance. He is strong and manly and brave. His voice may not be very beautiful, but it is sincere and fearless."

Everyone agreed this was not such a bad choice, so a delegation was sent to the rooster.

The rooster listened to the delegation. He was no braggart, but he had courage. Yet he hesitated.

"I don't think I can help you. The best I can do is cry 'cock-a-doodle-doo.' "

"Try it! Try it!" was the cry. "Maybe the sun will listen to you."

The next morning the rooster came early. He had begged the other birds to help him. Everybody wanted the sun to shine, so they all promised.

The rooster's feathers glistened even in the dark. The winds blew around his large red comb and he knew the importance of his task. An endless number of birds gathered near him. He stretched his neck toward the mountain and cried out with all his strength, "Cock-a-doodle-doo. . . . Cock-a-doodle-doo!"

The sun heard the strange cry. It was not sweet, but it was strong, sincere, and frank. The sun peeked out a little.

For the second time the rooster stood on his hard toes, stretched his neck high, spread his wings wide, and sang out, "Cock-a-doodle-doo; Cock-a-doodle-doo."

The sun heard it and his fear and anger began to wane. He peeped out a little more, but did not come out yet.

Once again the rooster stood high, wings spread wide, and cried pleadingly, "Cock-a-doodle-doo" three times. All the birds sang with him. It was truly a heavenly chorus.

The sun heard it and his anger and fear melted away. Slowly he came out from behind the mountain. And, as he came out, there came light and warmth that had not been there for a long time.

Everyone was happy now—the Hani people, the birds, the beasts, the sea, and the earth.

From that time on, the sun always comes out when the rooster crows three times and the birds join cock-a-doodle-doo with their songs.

# THE HEAVENLY SONG OF THE GREEN-SPOTTED DOVE

LISU

Listen with all your might, for then you may be lucky enough to hear the song of the Green-Spotted Dove to which the Lisu folks who live by the roaring Angry River listen with no end of joy. For the song of that dove brings to them the happiness of spring sunshine, life-giving rain, and rich growth in the valley and along the mountain-sides.

With the heavenly song of the Green-Spotted Dove, there is told a fanciful tale I will tell to you here.

In a village among the Lisu people there lived two families near each other. One was the family of a rich "mountain lord," and the other was the poor household of hard-working farmers. In each family there was a young son, both about the same age.

The two young men were friends. One day the rich young lord said to the other, "Let us build a raft of banana logs to go fishing," and the other agreed readily, and soon a raft was made and they were floating gayly down the river. Suddenly the rich young man saw a big carp gliding along.

"I must get this carp," shouted the rich young man, "I must get him!"

He pulled his sharp, long sword from his belt and threw it at the carp, but instead of hitting the fish, he struck the banana logs and cut the raft in two, leaving each young man on one half. For a time they drifted side by side, then the swirling water separated them.

The part with the young farmer came to a halt at a village—all empty! deserted! Not a human person, not an animal! He went from one empty hut to another! Suddenly he heard voices. Inside one of the houses he found a cupboard and two young women, quaking with fear, huddled together within it.

"Why are you hiding? Of what are you afraid? Where are all the people?"

"They ran away, those who lived! A terrible python and a fierce wild eagle killed almost everyone. Everyone who could, fled. We two were out in the woods picking herbs and were left behind. We were hiding here, for we were afraid the python and the eagle would come back and kill us."

"Have no fear! My sword and my arrow will destroy them."

No sooner were the words out of his mouth than a great golden-speckled python rushed at him wildly, followed by a giant eagle who swooped down from above, blocking out the sun and turning the sky dark. But with the courage of youth, the young man quickly dispatched the python with his sword and shot down the eagle with his arrow.

"Now I must continue to look for my lost friend," said the young farmer, "I cannot abandon him."

"You are a brave man, and we shall follow you to the end of the earth," the young girls said and got on the raft with him.

They went with him over many rivers and mountains. Each girl behaved according to her nature. The older one was vain and was dressed in fancy clothes, preening herself at every chance. But the younger was hard working and was dressed very simply. Since she did all the cooking, her face was besmudged most of the time with smoke hiding her lovely appearance.

While hunting in the forest one day, the young farmer almost shot a man rushing out of the woods. Imagine how overjoyed he was to discover that it was his long-lost friend. Laughing and weeping, the two friends hugged and embraced each other. They decided to start for home right away, taking the two sisters with them.

When the young mountain lord, who had not seen a woman for a long, long time, saw the elder girl so pretty and so nicely dressed, he offered to marry her at once. But the younger sister stayed with the poor young man and married him.

One day, after working in the field, she was returning home and stopped at a pond to wash the mud off her face. It happened that the rich young man was quietly fishing by the pond. When he saw her clean fresh face reflected in the water among the lotus blossoms, he was thunderstruck, for she was more beautiful than he had ever imagined or dreamed! Now he was sorry he had not married her instead of her sister, and he decided he would have her as a mistress, if only he could get rid of her husband.

The ungrateful friend thought about it and hit on a scheme. He invited the young farmer to go hunting with him. He led him through wild woods and valleys, promising him rich game until they came to the opening of a large cave on a cliff. A wind was blowing on the grass in front of it, making it look as if some wild beast was about to charge out of the cave.

The young mountain lord said, "A wild boar is coming out! Get it! Get it!"

The young farmer threw his spear with all his might.

He threw it so hard that he pitched into the cave and fell. He fell and fell for a long time, for it was a magic cave. When he finally landed, he found himself surrounded by little ant people. They were the inhabitants of the Kingdom of Ants. They were clearing the fields to plant crops, but, being so small, it took them a long, long time to do what he could do with one stroke of the sword. So he began to help them, swinging his long sword.

In no time at all the fields were cleared. The King of Ants was pleased, but he was also worried that this giant helper would eat too much. The ungrateful King ordered the young farmer kept captive in the cave.

He said, "Now you will be our prisoner and work for us as a slave. You will work in the fields and will not be permitted to speak to anyone or leave our cave."

But some of the ant people felt sorry for the young farmer and from time to time brought him food. He also caught animals in the cave and kept himself alive.

Day after day he worked. His life was very sad. He longed for his home and his lovely wife. With those unhappy thoughts and yearnings he made a bamboo flute and put into it the music of his heart's longing and sadness and hopes. It was truly heavenly music.

All the animals who heard the music of that flute were enchanted by it. A crow came and promised to lead him home in exchange for the flute. But as soon as the crow got the flute, he flew to the top of a tree to sing with his new voice and forgot all about his bargain. A kindly ant climbed up on the branches and bit the crow hard on the tail.

"Ouch!" croaked the crow. The flute fell out of his beak, and the young man quickly picked it up.

Then a porcupine came and offered to make a tunnel through the mountain so that the young man could escape. He, too, wanted to have the flute, and the young man agreed, for he had only one thought—to go home! The porcupine huffed and puffed and dug and dug so hard that . . . "poop!", he passed wind right in the face of the young man, who was behind him.

"Phew!" cried the young man, holding his nose. At his cry, the whole tunnel caved in. Again, he could not go home.

One day the Green-Spotted Dove came and offered to wing him back to his village if he would give her the flute. The young man gladly agreed.

The Green-Spotted Dove called many of her bird friends and told them to get on top of a bamboo tree. They bent the branches way down to the ground and asked the young man to hold on.

"Now get hold of them," said the Green-Spotted Dove. The young man did. Then the birds flew off all at once, and the branches sprang up, flinging the young man all the way to his village.

He found his hut overgrown with weeds, and in the distance he heard his wife weeping. She had driven off the offers of the rich young man and so he had tied her with ropes and imprisoned her in his house.

Her true young husband rushed to her side, cut the ropes with his sword, and rescued her. He was so happy and his heart was so filled with song that he no longer needed his flute. Instead, he gave his flute and the beautiful song in it to the Green-Spotted Dove as a reward for what she had done for him.

The two, the poor young man and his lovely wife, lived happily ever after, and the Green-Spotted Dove put the lovely song into her heart and has sung it ever since, bringing happiness, sunshine, and spring to the Lisu people of Yunnan.

TAI

# THE
# WHITE-HAIR
# WATERFALL

TUNG

High up where the Tung people live, there is a mountain called Tou-kao Shan, which means "The Steep High Mountain." Midway to the peak of this mountain a rushing waterfall comes cascading down, looking like white hair flowing over someone's shoulder. The waterfall brings clear sweet water to those who live in the village nearby and to birds and beasts as well. It brings refreshing pleasure to all. Folks call it the White-Hair Waterfall and from it floats a strange tale that happened in the dim far years.

Long ago there were no streams on that mountain, and the people had to wait for the rains from Heaven to give them the much-needed water; and when the heat of the sun dried up the Heaven, folks had to travel full seven *li*\* to get it.

\* A *li* is about one-third of a mile.

Now, in the village at the foot of that high peak lived a girl who had the longest hair anyone had ever seen. It was beautiful blue-black in color and reached nearly to her ankles. She would pile most of it on top of her head, and what was still left she would wind around her neck and shoulders, often using it almost as a cloak. The villagers called her the "Long-Hair Girl."

She lived with her old mother who could not walk. Long-Hair Girl took good care of her and of their home. She worked hard in the house and in the garden and in the field, finding food for the young pigs they kept.

One day, while looking for plants to feed the pigs, she walked high up on the mountain and noticed some long, thick, jagged radish leaves growing out among the rocks.

"Those will make a fine meal for my pigs," she said aloud. She began tugging at the leaves and soon out came a big red radish, and from the hole made there gushed out a stream of clear fresh water.

She was thirsty, so she took a long drink. It tasted sweet, and she drank for a long time. When she was through she heaved a deep sigh of pleasure. At the same moment a strong wind came up, whipped the radish out of her hand, and plugged it into the hole from which the water had gushed, closing it tight.

The wind became stronger and lifted the girl and carried her along the peak, setting her down at an opening that led to a cave. She looked around and soon she saw a man all covered with yellow hair sitting on the ground. He looked angry.

"Long-Hair Girl," he said in a deep voice, "you have learned the secret of my sweet-water spring! I am the Spirit of the Mountain, and this spring is mine; I have guarded it for many years. Now you know it. Keep it secret. If you tell anyone, you will lose your life. Remember that!"

Again, the wind blew strongly, lifted Long-Hair Girl

from the mouth of the cave, and carried her to her village in front of her home.

She did not tell anyone the secret of the spring. When she saw friends and neighbors struggling on the rocky roads, carrying heavy buckets on shoulder poles to bring precious water from the little river seven *li* away, her heart was filled with pity and sorrow. She could not eat or sleep. She fell silent and her pink cheeks paled. Her beautiful blue-black hair that was the pride of her life turned snow white.

One day she saw an old man struggling over rocks with two buckets of water he had carried a long way. Suddenly the old man's foot hit a boulder and he fell. The buckets dropped from his shoulder pole and turned over, spilling all the precious water. The old man's hand and face were cut and bleeding.

The sight was too much for Long-Hair Girl. Her heart was filled with black misery. She forgot all warning of danger from the yellow-haired Spirit of the Mountain.

"Don't worry about your lost water, Grandfather!" she cried. "There is all the water you need right nearby, right here on the mountainside near our village. I will take you to it. It is guarded jealously by the Spirit of the Mountain, but I know the secret and I will tell it to you and the whole village, though it be my death!"

Having revealed the secret, she felt suddenly relieved. She ran all over the village, shouting, "Come, follow me! All you have to do is pull out the radish and destroy it. There is a spring on the Steep High Mountain! I saw it with my own eyes!" She began running up the mountain to the place where the big radish leaves sprouted. The old man and some neighbors who were near followed her.

She came to the jagged leaves. "Come," she cried, "help me pull out the radish and chop it up quickly!"

They all pulled with a good will and soon the big red radish came out, and with it . . . a stream of cool fresh water.

"Quick!" she cried. "Cut the radish to pieces so that it

cannot close the spring again. Quick!" Everyone went at it with his kitchen knife, rock, or stick, while the water kept on flowing.

"Now," she added, "make the opening wide and more water will flow." They all did this with their hands and whatever tools they had. A great mass of water now rushed from the spring.

But at that moment a wild gust of wind carried Long-Hair Girl away, taking her to the cave where the Spirit of the Mountain covered with yellow hair, sat glowering. He was blazing with anger and shouted fiercely at her:

"You betrayed my secret! I will punish you for it by laying you over the cliff at the spring, so that the ice-cold water will always spill over you, and you will suffer forever."

Long-Hair Girl had lost all fear and she answered courageously, "I am willing to suffer for the sake of my relatives and friends in the village. But I ask one favor: Let me return to my home for a short time to find someone to take care of my old mother!"

"You may go," Spirit of the Mountain answered, "but come back quickly or I will destroy the whole village."

A strong wind came along again and carried Long-Hair Girl to her very home. The story had reached there already, and friends and neighbors wholeheartedly promised to help.

It was hard for Long-Hair Girl to leave her mother, whom she loved dearly. She caressed her over and over, but did not tell her that she would never see her again. She said she was going to visit a friend who lived in the next village and she might not come back for a long time.

She petted her little pigs whom she had been feeding, and when she walked up the mountain and passed her favorite banyan tree under which she had rested so often, she stopped and patted the trunk with her hands and said with tears in her voice, "Never again will I rest in your generous shade, my lovely tree!"

At those words a tall old man came from behind the

tree. He had green hair and a green beard and his clothes were all deep green too.

"Lovely Long-Hair Girl," he said, "where are you going and why are you crying?" Long-Hair Girl was silent. She sighed and hung her head.

The old man said, "I already know about you. For your kind thoughts and good deed I will save you! I knew you would come this way. Now, look what I have done." He pulled from under the leaves a stone statue that was the image of Long-Hair Girl except for one thing—it had no hair on the head.

"I made it, and now I will take the white hair from your head and put it on the stone head. The Spirit of the Mountain will believe it is you, but it will be the stone statue that will take the eternal punishment of cold water instead."

Long-Hair Girl took the white hair from her head and put it on the stone head where it took root at once.

The tall old man in green lifted the stone statue and took it up the mountain to the spring. There he laid it face downward so that the cold water fell over the long white hair, making of it a long white waterfall.

Suddenly Long-Hair Girl felt a strange prickling on her head . . . where the white hair had been there was a new growth of blue-black hair such as she had had before!

She found herself standing under her beloved banyan tree from which the man in green had come to help her by the power of his magic. He was not there, but his voice came from the tree: "Go home, Long-Hair Girl. Go to your mother whom you love and to your friends for whom you were ready to give your life. Go to them to share their joy and happiness."

And she did just that.

# THE STORY OF THE HOUSE

SHUI

水

Why! Why! Why!
Why do people live in houses?
Why do animals live in the woods and on the hill?
Why do dragons live in the black sea?

The Shui people of China have an answer to these questions.

Endless years ago, so far that even the most ancient ancestors cannot remember, there were mountains everywhere and people lived in caves, together with animals and birds.

One day the sky turned as black as night, without stars, and a roaring storm came up. Wild winds howled, torrents of rain pelted the earth, and hail as big as nuts pounded everywhere. A screaming wind tore trees from the earth and flung rocks around like pebbles. Mountains fell, animals and men were destroyed. All, all perished except three creatures: a young man, a tiger, and a dragon.

The three had hidden beneath a giant rock too big to be lifted by the winds, and so they were saved.

The waters surged around them and the winds blew cold. All the caves were flooded, and the three could not return to their homes. They huddled together to keep warm.

"We must do something to remain alive," said the young man.

"Yes we must," growled Tiger and Dragon.

"We must build a house," said the young man.

"Let us start right away," roared Tiger.

Tiger rushed out and began looking for dry grasses and twigs. Dragon leaped around for logs and rolled them to one place, where the young man used stones as knives and vines as ropes to cut and bind the logs and thatches.

So, working hard, they soon had a house built where it was dry and warm. There they lived willingly with one another—but not for long. Tiger and Dragon each wanted the house for himself, but neither would say so outright.

They began arguing and fighting. Things got worse and worse, and in the end they all cried they could not live together.

"Only one of us can stay in the house," said the young man.

"Let us have a test to see which one can keep the others out of the house. The one who wins will keep it." This from Tiger.

"Agreed," cried the other two. "Those who can't stay in the house must get out!"

"I will try first," roared Tiger. "I'll get you two out!"

He leaped out of the house, shaking his tail, destroying grass and trees around him and roaring with all his might. Wild echoes answered back; sand flew and rocks fell like hail, but the young man and Dragon huddled in the corner of the house, scared but not frightened enough to run outside.

Tiger was tired. He stopped and came back into the house.

"Now I will try," shrilled Dragon.

He lumbered out on his clawed legs and began piling black clouds in the sky. He bellowed and zished and let loose thunder and lightning and created a downpour. It sounded as if the world were ending. It was truly fearful, but the young man and Tiger, though frightened, were not frightened enough to run away. They clung to each other and stayed in the house.

The storm ended, and Dragon, exhausted, came in, looking at the two in anger.

"Now it is my chance," said the young man. "I cannot roar or shake my tail. I cannot stir up black clouds or bring thunder and hail, but I will use just a little flame."

He went out the door, took two stones and, rubbing them together, created a small flame and put it to some dry grass on the house, and started it burning. As the grass burned, a wisp of smoke wafted inside. Tiger and Dragon sniffed. They heard the crackling of the fire. Like a shot, they dashed outside.

Tiger ran into the forest on the hills and Dragon ran into the sea where there was no smoke. The young man put out his little fire and ran into the house.

Tiger liked the forest on the hills.

Dragon liked the sea.

The young man liked the house.

And there they have stayed ever since, each liking his own home, where he is free from the others.

# THE
# TALE
# OF THE
# MAGIC GREEN
# WATER-PEARL

NUNG
農

On the southern border of Yunnan Province there is a flat land surrounded by mountains with wild flowers, pines, and bamboos. It is rich with growth-giving water pouring from the mountaintop and warmth-giving sunshine pouring from Heaven. The earth is thick black, and fruit-laden palm and banana trees and nourishing grain and vegetables are there in great plenty for men and beasts. And all this, thanks to the Green Water-Pearl. Here is the tale of the Green Water-Pearl as told by the old folks of the Nung tribe.

Years and years ago there was in that place a village where people lived in wooden two-storied houses and worked very hard. One clear and starry night in the autumn harvest season the old folks were sitting around the fire pit to keep warm; children were playing games, and young folks were making plans for happy days. Suddenly there was an ear-split-ting roll of thunder, a wild flare in the sky, and from high above there streaked down a flaming rock—a meteor, bringing with it wild spluttering flames. The fire covered the whole village, burning both houses and people. There was wild screaming, and those who could, fled in terror.

The burning continued, and those fortunate to escape took refuge in the mountains. The valley burned for days and months and years, and the refugees could not return home. The fertile land turned into scorched earth where nothing would grow. What made it worse for the few who had escaped was that one year there was a terrible drought on the mountain where they had built their new homes. No rain; only hot, hot sunshine. The fruits, berries, vegetables all died. The villagers suffered terribly. This went on and on and there was no end in sight.

Now, among those who had escaped was a young man named Yen-kang, who lived with his old mother in a little hut. Next to them lived a neighbor he called Uncle Lu and his daughter Lo-ying, who was Yen-kang's bride-to-be. He loved Lo-ying and he also loved his shining shoulder pole. This was made of speckled bamboo, smooth and gleaming in the sunshine like gold. He never went anywhere without it.

One day Yen-kang said to Uncle Lu and the two women, "Let us leave this barren dry place and find a home where life will not be so hard."

"Son," Uncle Lu answered, "where is life easy? Where you see the burning valley, there was once a fine village. Then, one evening, a fiery meteor fell from Heaven and everything became different. The meteor kept on burning without stopping. We fled from the fire, but we have not found any place with food where we can live peacefully. I don't think we will find anything better, though an old shaman told us years ago that life would be happy for us again if we could get the Green Water-Pearl to help us."

"The Green Water-Pearl! Where is it?" asked Yen-kang.

"Son, far away in the east there is the Spring Mountain. On that mountain there is a deep pond, and in that pond lies the Green Water-Pearl. Only the Water-Pearl can put out the fire of our village, and then we can live there again. But it cannot be. A fierce golden spider guards that pearl day and night. The only way to destroy the spider is with the golden stinger that is in the belly of Old King Bee. He lives in another mountain in the west called Flower Mountain, which is covered by no end of flowers always surrounded by thousands of bees. Two of our young men have tried to get the Water-Pearl, but one died on the way and the other died as soon as he came back. We never found out why they failed."

"I will try," said Yen-kang, "and I will come back with the Green Water-Pearl to give us the happiness we had before." His mother and his future wife begged him not to go, but he only repeated what he had said: "I am going to get the Green Water-Pearl and I will succeed."

The next morning his mother gave him freshly baked bread, and she and all the village bade him good luck and good-by. Yen-kang set out to the mountain in the west. Soon he came to a meadow covered with more flowers than he had ever seen, and around the flowers zoomed swarms of bees busy gathering pollen for honey. King Bee was in a hive in the middle, with hordes of bees around to protect him. Yen-kang could not get near. As he stood there wondering what to do, he saw an eagle high in the sky dive down to a crow's nest, pick up one of the young birds in his claws, and fly off. The mother crow tried desperately to rescue her child but did not have the speed or the strength to do so. Yen-kang quickly took his smooth golden shoulder pole and threw it with all his strength at the eagle—and hit him! The eagle dropped the young crow and flew off.

The mother bird flew to Yen-kang and thanked him again and again for saving her child. Said she, "If there is anything I can do for you, just tell me and I will."

"I wonder if you could tell me how to get the golden

sting from King Bee. The bees around him don't let me near him."

"That's easy," said the mother crow.

She crowed several times and, from all sides, crows came flying by the hundreds. The mother crow cawed out an order to them and at once they began to gather dry straw, leaves, and twigs, putting them in a pile over the Flower Mountain. Yen-kang struck a rock with his shiny shoulder pole until sparks began flying, setting the grass, the leaves, and the twigs on fire and bringing up a heavy thick smoke. The bees flew from the smoke, leaving Old King Bee alone in the hive. Yen-kang whacked the beehive with his shoulder pole, and Old King Bee flew out and disappeared into the air. But the mother crow flew around and soon brought Old King Bee back in her beak, and Yen-kang plucked the golden stinger from the bee's belly.

He took it quickly to the eastern Spring Mountain, straight to the big pond surrounded by thin-leaved willow trees. At the end of the pond was an underwater cave with the Green Water-Pearl in it. The opening of the cave was covered by a heavy web spun by the golden spider. Yen-kang tried to break through it with his carrying pole, but he was caught. The golden spider crawled over and tried to swallow him, but, using his free hand, Yen-kang stabbed him with King Bee's golden stinger and overcame him. He freed himself from the web and rushed into the cave. There in the center lay the beautiful Green Water-Pearl! He picked it up, but it was so cold, his fingers froze. Without thinking, Yen-kang popped it into his mouth and it slid down his throat into his stomach, but it was so icy that he lost consciousness.

While he was unconscious something strange and magical happened to Yen-kang. When he awoke he had become a giant, and a rushing stream of water came from his mouth. He rose, pushed rocks and trees aside, and climbed up the big mountain. There he lay down and the magic water poured right into the valley where the fire was still raging.

The water put out the fire, and Yen-kang turned into a mountain range. His mouth became a cave out of which rushed a big river that ran across the middle of the valley, bringing good water and growth to man and animals. It made everything green, as it had been in the olden, olden days.

The people named the mountain the Yen-kang Mountain and the river Yen-kang River, and, with the help of the sweet water, the village was again a happy place.

# THE WONDERFUL CHUANG BROCADE

CHUANG

壮

For thousands of years the people of China have been famous for their rich art in silken brocades. The Chuang people of Kwangsi Province are especially well known for their beautiful designs and pictures. Some of them tell stories such as this one.

In this province, at the foot of high peaks, in a thatched cottage, lived an old widow with her three sons: Lemo, Letui, and Leju. The old mother was a most wonderful weaver of brocades, which merchants and folks bought from her to make vests, bedcovers, and blankets. Her sons were woodcutters.

One day the old mother went to sell a fine brocade she had made. In the merchant's shop hung a painting of wondrous beauty. It showed a village with a rich, tall palace with colorful gardens around it. Beautiful flowers and ripe vegetables were everywhere; ducks, chickens and cows were all over. Never had she seen a more beautiful scene. Quickly she sold her brocade and bought the painting, forgetting rice and other foods she needed.

At home she proudly showed the painting. "How happy I would be to live in that palace with its gardens," she said to her sons.

"That is a dream, Ah-mee*," spoke Lemo, the oldest son.

"Maybe we will live in such a place in our next life," said Letui, her second son.

Then Leju, the youngest said, "Ah-mee, you must weave a brocade just like the painting, and when you look at your work you will think you are living in the palace with those gardens."

"You are right, son," said the old mother, and she set to work at once.

Day in, day out, and nights as well, she worked at the wooden loom with silk threads, and the scene of the painting grew in beauty on the brocade.

She never stopped working. Her old eyes hurt from the smoke of the pine-oil lamps, but she did not stop. After one year, tears filled her eyes, but instead of stopping, she put her tears into the brocade and made of them a singing river and a shining pond full of fishes. After two years, drops of blood fell from her eyes onto the brocade. Out of these she wove bright red flowers and a glowing sun.

So the old near-blind mother worked for three years until she finished putting the painting into the brocade. The sons were so proud of her work, they took it out of their dark hut and put it in front of the door where there was enough daylight to see and admire it. Everyone who saw it exclaimed, "What a wonderful Chuang brocade!"

All of a sudden a weird whirring wind came along and

* Ah-mee is the word for "mother" in Chuang language.

. . . whisht! it picked up the brocade and carried it high, high up into the sky and . . . the brocade disappeared.

The old mother fainted, everyone shouted . . . but the brocade was gone. The mother became very ill and no doctor could help her. She was forever crying for her brocade!

Seeing this, Lemo said, "Mother, stop grieving! I will find your beautiful brocade and bring it back to you."

"Go, son, and may good fortune go with you."

Lemo set out over mountains and across rivers. One day he came to a mountain pass, on one side of which stood a stone house. To the right was a stone horse, its mouth wide open, bent over an arbutus bush full of red berries.

At the door sat an old white-haired woman.

"Who are you and where are you going, young man?" she asked Lemo.

He told her the tale of his mother's beautiful brocade— how hard and long she had worked at it and how the wind had carried it away, and how very ill she had become.

"Young Lemo, I know all this. The winds of the mountains tell me many things. Your brocade is now in the Sun Mountain of the East with the beautiful fairies who live there. They saw the brocade and sent the wind for it. They are now copying your mother's beautiful work, and you can get it back only with the help of the stone horse. But the horse will help you only if you give him two of your teeth for the ones he is missing in his mouth so that he can eat the berries from the arbutus bush. Then he will take you far and wide to the Sun Mountain in the East.

"On the way you will come to a mountain of leaping flames through which you must pass. You must do it in silence and without fear. If you cry out even once, you will turn into charcoal.

"Then you will come to a sea full of jagged ice with knife-cutting cold winds tearing at you, but you must not cry out or even shiver with cold. If you do, you will be crushed by the wild tossing ice and buried in the icy water.

"If you go through these trials, you will get your mother's brocade."

Lemo was silent. His face turned blue with fear and he hung his head and thought—for a long time. To lose his teeth and endure such terrible trials!

The old woman watched him. Then she said, "Son, your face tells your thoughts. It says: it is too much! But you tried, so here is a little iron box full of gold nuggets. Go back home and live well."

Lemo took the box and thanked her and left. But he was still thinking hard. "If I go home I must share the gold with all my family! There will be little for me. . . . No! I will go to the city and live on my wealth!" So he turned his steps toward the big city.

The old mother waited and waited, pining for her beautiful brocade. "If only I could see it before I die," she cried continually.

Letui, her second son, said, "Mother, I will bring you your brocade," and he set off at once.

He, too, came to the stone house with the old lady and her stone horse, and she told him just what she had told Lemo.

Letui also thought and thought, and the old woman knew what was in his mind. "Son," she said, "I can tell you think the trials are too much for you, but you started bravely, so here is a little iron box with gold nuggets. Go back and live happily." But Letui thought as did Lemo, so instead of going home, he too turned toward the city.

At home the old mother waited, crying for her handiwork until her eyes gave out and she became completely blind!

Leju, the youngest son, said, "Mother, I will go on the road to find your beautiful brocade and bring it back to you. You will be with kind neighbors who will take care of you while I am away."

He bade her good cheer and went off. Like his brothers,

he came to the stone house with the stone horse and the old woman. She told him how he could get the brocade only with the help of the horse, and of the dangers he must face.

Instead of thinking long as his brothers had, Leju gave two of his teeth to the horse and mounted it. The horse ate the berries and then went off swift as the wind. Horse and rider went through the burning mountain and the icy sea. But Leju sat firm on the horse, thinking only of helping his mother, and so he reached the Sun Mountain and the palace where the lovely fairies were busy copying *Ah-mee's* masterpiece.

Leju spoke to them, telling them of his mother's sickness and blindness, and of how she continued to cry for her lost brocade.

"We will finish copying your mother's wonderful work by tomorrow morning," said one of the maidens. "Then you can take it back to your *Ah-mee*."

They gave him delicious fruits to eat, and he fell asleep. But during the night the fairies hung a big glowing pearl on the rafter and wove by its light.

A maiden in a red dress finished first. She looked at her own work, and then at *Ah-mee's*. She sighed, "I'm afraid mine is not nearly as fine. I wish I could live in the beautiful place that is on *her* brocade." So she began weaving her own image right near the fish pond that *Ah-mee* had woven.

Leju slept in the palace of the fairies, but the next morning, before the maidens arose, he took his mother's brocade, mounted the stone horse, and in the wink of time they were back at the stone house where the white-haired woman sat waiting for him.

"Leju, your mother is very ill," she said. "Hurry back. The sight of her brocade will bring her health." Then she took the two teeth from the horse's mouth and put them back into Leju's. Next she put a pair of magic deerskin shoes on his feet and bade him good luck.

The shoes were like wings and took him swiftly to his home, where his mother was lying in bed, thin as a stick and barely alive.

"Ah-mee," he shouted, "I have brought you your brocade. Here!"

No sooner did she touch it than she began to feel well again. Her eyes opened wide and once again she could see! She got up and took her beloved work out into the open sunshine and then . . . a miracle happened! The embroidery of her brocade became a real place. Trees! Flowers! All were there before the rich palace, and by the fish pond stood the lovely maiden in her red dress.

Leju married the maiden, and the two lived happily all their lives.

One day two beggars came to their village. They were Lemo and Letui. They had spent all their gold, drinking, eating, and making merry in the city, and now they were dressed in rags and begging for food. When they saw the beautiful garden where Ah-mee, Leju, and his wife were walking and singing, they quietly slipped away, too ashamed to face their mother and brother.

# THE GREAT BATTLE BETWEEN THE GRASSHOPPERS AND THE MONKEYS

PUYI 布依

In the dim gray past of long ago, life was different than it is today. Then animals spoke to one another as people did. They argued and battled just as men do.

Let me tell you what happened in the strange battle between the monkeys and the hopping grasshoppers.

The grasshoppers lived in the fields and valleys as they do today, and the monkeys lived in the mountains as they do now. One day, the monkeys decided it would be nicer to live in the warm valley than in the cool mountains. So the chief of monkeys came down to the chief of grasshoppers and said, "You grasshoppers are little, hopping around in a big valley too large for you. You can live just as well in the mountains filled with woods. We monkeys are big and heavy and need space to spread. We want to live in the fields and valleys, and you go into the mountains."

Chirped the chief of grasshoppers, "We were all born in these fields and we have lived our life here and here we will stay."

Chattered the monkey, "No, you won't."

"Yes, we will."

Said the monkey, "If you want to stay here, you must fight for the right! We challenge you to a fight, and the ones who win can stay in the fields!"

The grasshoppers, feeling themselves the weaker, had to accept, so they shrilled, "We agree. Come tomorrow morning and we'll battle with you."

Early the next morning, the monkeys came from the mountains armed with sticks and thick tree twigs. No grasshoppers were there.

"Come out, you green grasshoppers, and fight for your fields," they shouted.

The leader of the grasshoppers shouted back, "You must wait until the sun is up. The dew is very heavy and we are all dripping wet. As soon as we are dry, we will fight."

The sun came up warm and friendly and dried the grasshoppers. The monkeys felt the sun too, so they shouted, "Are you ready?"

"Yes, we are," shrilled the leader of the grasshoppers, and with that he took one great hop, landing on the nose of the chief of monkeys.

"There is a grasshopper on your nose, chief," cried the monkey standing next to him. "I'll get him." With that he lifted the heavy stick in his hand and, aiming at the nose of his chief on which the enemy stood, he hit him a fierce blow. So strong was the blow that he squashed the nose deep between the eyes. And there it has remained ever since.

As for the battle, the grasshoppers kept leaping on the noses of the monkeys, while the monkeys kept on hitting their own wildly to drive them off, and so knocked down their own kind. Soon the valley was strewn with unconscious monkeys.

"Who wins?" chirped and shrilled the hopping grasshoppers.

The monkeys who could speak answered weakly, "You win! you win! Keep your valleys and fields; we will stay in our safe mountains."

And so it has been ever since. The grasshoppers live in the fields, and the monkeys in the mountains.

# THE
# GOD
# OF FACES

TAI

Once upon a time there lived in Monbanasi Village by the wild Salween River a man by the name of Tolanwa. His little bamboo pavilion was in a coconut grove surrounded by flowers. The little home seesawed with the singing winds, but that never bothered him. He sat all day at the bamboo window watching the swaying flowers and flying birds.

Every day he was there, except on days of temple celebrations. Then he put his many-colored blanket on his shoulders and walked to the noisy Buddhist temple. Not so much to pray or to listen to the music made by gongs and drums or to watch the ceremonies of sprinkling water—he only went to look at the faces of worshipers praying and chanting. When they were finished and the temple candles were snuffed out, Tolanwa went back to his little bamboo home to paint on flower petals and bamboo leaves the faces he had seen in the temple. He loved painting, and his work showed the love he put into it.

He painted seven faces each day and night for seven days and nights until he had painted forty-nine faces. Then he copied them on paper, cloth, and satin and sold them to the good wayfaring pilgrims.

Of course he could never sell all of them, since he was forever painting more new faces as he saw them. After ten years his little home hardly had enough room for his work, but he kept on painting just the same.

One wild, windy night when he was at work painting the most beautiful girl on earth, there was a tapping at his door.

"Come in," cried Tolanwa. The door swung open and in came a tall man, a black shawl over his shoulders and a black turban wound around his head. Tolanwa greeted him, adding, "It is a poor night for traveling when even owls stay home."

The man was silent for a few minutes. Then he spoke in a deep voice: "I am a messenger from the Heavenly King. I am the God of Death and I have come to take you with me."

Tolanwa shuddered, but kept on painting the beautiful face. Then he said, "The gods must be obeyed, but please, God of Death, go back to the Heavenly King and tell him that I am busy painting the face of the most beautiful girl on earth and I would like to finish it."

"That I cannot do," said the God of Death and walked up to Tolanwa where he sat working.

He looked at the painting. Truly, even though unfinished, it was of wondrous beauty. "I would like to see it finished," he said, "and I will ask the Heavenly King to grant your request."

He returned to the Heavenly King and said, "King of Heaven, Tolanwa is at work painting the most beautiful face on earth, but he needs time to finish it. When he is done I will bring him to you."

The King of Heaven was angry when he heard this and he thundered, "You must bring him here before the stars fade out of the sky."

The God of Death returned to the jungle to the village of coconut trees, to the bamboo hut where Tolanwa still sat painting the beautiful face, and he whispered to him the mes- sage of the King of Heaven.

Tolanwa put some finishing touches to the lovely face. Then he gathered together as many paintings as he could carry, lighted two candles as a sign of respect, and, holding them, he followed the God of Death. So he came before the King of Heaven. The King looked at the paintings by the light of the two candles, and a friendly smile spread over his face.

"Tolanwa," he said, "you are a famous painter in the land and I can see why. Now you will stay with me and I will make you the God of Faces. You will sit with the God of Birth and help him in his task."

There he still sits, and every time the God of Birth is ready to send a soul to the earth, Tolanwa whips out one of his paintings and gives it to the soul, which keeps it for life.

But Tolanwa is a selfish god and does not like to give away the most beautiful faces he has painted, so when a Tai woman expects a child, she prays to Tolanwa and brings him offerings of fresh beautiful flowers so that he will give her child one of the beautiful faces he has set aside for the ones he specially favors.

# THE PEACOCK'S TAIL

MIAO

苗

Once, long ago, when the animals in the forest in the mountains were like folks living in villages and towns, they spoke and argued just like people.

One day one of the Immortals in Heaven looked down into a forest on a high mountain where many animals were playing and grazing.

"I think I can make their life happier by making them more beautiful," thought the Immortal.

So he floated down from Heaven among the animals and greeted them and said, "I am one of the Immortals from Heaven and have come to help you. If there is any among you who thinks he is ugly and would like to look better, say so and I will do my best to change him."

The animals all stood silent, just looking at one another. Here was something they had never thought of. Not one had ever questioned his looks. The monkey stood nearest to the Immortal, and the Immortal asked:

"You, Monkey, are you satisfied with your appearance? People often laugh at you."

"Let them laugh," the monkey said, "it does not bother me. I think I am nice-looking. I have nimble legs I can use as well as my hands, and I have a nice long tail. I can swing from tree to tree as fast as a bird can fly. I am much better than that horse standing next to me. He is ten, twenty times as big as I am, with a tail thicker and bushier than mine, swishing and swooshing for no reason, and a face silly and long. His looks can surely be improved."

The horse felt deeply insulted and gave the monkey a few kicks. Then he said, "I think I look fine and strong, and my head is quite handsome. My tail is useful for driving away flies. If you want to take away some ugliness, there is the elephant. His body is too big, his legs too fat, his nose is the longest in the world, and his tail is silly and thin and useless. Do something for him, O Immortal! He needs it."

This made the elephant very angry. He sprayed the horse with streams of water from his nose and whipped around wildly with his skinny tail. Then he began stomping around with his heavy legs, splashing mud and water on everyone near him.

"I am beautiful enough," he shouted in his trumpeting voice. "No one can make me more beautiful. My strength is my beauty. But look, O Immortal from Heaven," and he pointed to a frightened peacock sitting shivering on the branch of a tree. "Look at that poor bird without a noble nose. His head looks like an old worthless copper kettle, and his wings are blue and black like the wings of a rotting dead crow. His tail is stubby as a brush. He is ugly enough to need help from Heaven."

The peacock jumped down from the branch and said humbly, "True, Immortal from high Heaven, I have no legs like the monkey, or a swishing tail like the horse, or a body or

a nose like the grand elephant. I have nothing of which I can be proud, and my tail is short and stumpy and ugly, and I am ashamed to show it. Truly, Immortal, if you could do something to make me a little more beautiful, I would thank you with praises to reach Heaven."

The Immortal's eyes gleamed with pleasure at the humble plea of the peacock. "Good bird, modesty begets rewards. I will help you. I will give you beauty that no bird has. I will give you a tail that will be fitting for a jade palace. I will take away the stump of feathers and give you a tail of long feathers that will spread out to look like jewels. Each feather will end in a brilliant black eye more lovely than the eyes of a beautiful princess in the palace of the Emperor."

As all the animals watched, the Immortal plucked out the stump of feathers from the peacock's tail and with heavenly magic put in wondrously beautiful new feathers.

And there they have stayed ever since.

The Immortal flew up to Heaven, and the peacock flew up the tree and spread out his beautiful tail for all the animals to see. Truly it gleamed like jewels in the jade palace of an emperor.

The animals secretly admired and envied the heavenly gift the peacock received for his modesty.

# TURKIC

# SMART HEAD
# BETTER THAN
# SHARP TEETH

KAZAKH

哈薩克

Kazakh shepherds who live in northern Sinkiang, a Chinese province near Soviet Russia, sometimes hunt by making deep traps rather than tracking animals on horseback with the help of dogs. They sell the fur pelts to earn extra money.

One warm sunny day, a Kazakh set out on a hunt. He came to a narrow path on the edge of a deep wood where he knew animals passed on their way to a spring. He dug a deep hole in the path, then he criss-crossed the hole with twigs and branches and covered them with grass and dirt so the trap would not be seen. He was pleased with his work and went back to his tent, planning to return the next day.

But all the time a gray monkey sitting on a branch of a cypress tree had been watching the Kazakh hunter at work.

"I will stay up here," chattered Monkey to himself, "and see who falls first into that trap."

145

It did not take much time when there came along the narrow path a mother rabbit looking for food for her young ones. She was heading straight for the trap.

Monkey felt pity for Mother Rabbit and did not want to see her trapped. So Monkey screeched, "Stop! Stop! Don't walk! Where are you going?"

"I am looking for new green grass for food to feed my little rabbits born two days ago," piped Mother Rabbit.

"If you walk farther on that path you will be food for the hunter. He dug a trap right on that path."

"Thank you! Thank you a thousand times. I will tell all my children of your goodness."

Rabbit turned from the path and took a detour into the woods and ran right into—the open mouth of a hungry wolf!

"Good day, good Rabbit, and most welcome! You look very appetizing and I am very hungry. You will make a fine meal for me."

"Please! please! Have pity! I have many hungry little children waiting at home for me, and I am looking for food for them. Please! please! Find someone fatter than I am. I am only hair and bones."

"Oh, no, you will be just right. I am as hungry as your children and you will make a good meal."

Mother Rabbit was desperate; she thought this was very unfair, and she wanted the opinion of another animal.

Right then, Fox, a friend of Wolf, passed by. He had heard their words.

"Yes, Rabbit will make a good meal for Wolf. She ought to let Wolf eat her," said Fox.

"I am glad, friend Fox, that you agree with me. You know my appetite is bigger than all the little rabbits this rabbit ever had, and you are a good judge, Fox."

Rabbit though Fox very biased. She wanted a really fair judge. Wolf agreed to try again.

They found Monkey. He had just climbed down from

a tree to see what was happening. Said Wolf to Monkey, "You, Monkey, must agree with Fox that I am superior to Rabbit and have the right to eat her."

"It isn't fair," cried shivering Rabbit, "it isn't fair."

"How are you better than Rabbit?" Monkey asked Wolf.

Wolf answered quickly, "I have sharp teeth that could finish an ox, four powerful legs that could outrun an antelope—"

"Wait," said Monkey, "how do we know you can really run so fast? Here is an idea. Why not put you to a test? Why don't you run a race with Rabbit? If you win, you can eat Rabbit. If you lose, Rabbit is free to go. But Wolf is heavier than Rabbit, so Wolf can begin twenty feet ahead of Rabbit."

"No question Wolf will win!" cried Fox, "Even I can win this race."

Monkey smiled, "Why don't you join, too? Maybe you can get Rabbit's ears."

Wolf readily agreed to let Fox join in the race.

"The race must be run on this narrow path, and that cypress tree is the finishing point," pointed Monkey.

"Now, line up: you, Wolf, first," and he led him to the path directly before the trap. "Now, you, Fox, stand right by Wolf, and you, Rabbit, get twenty feet behind them."

"When I whistle," said Monkey, "you, Wolf and Fox, start off as fast as you can. And you, Rabbit, do the same."

Monkey whistled and screamed, "Go!"

Wolf and Fox started off strongly on the narrow path, and in a few minutes both fell into the trap. But Mother Rabbit stayed behind safely. She and the Monkey laughed and laughed, then she thanked Monkey again and again and ran off happily to find food for her children.

Monkey shook his head and mumbled, "Big teeth, big mouth, but empty head."

# ANIZU'S MAGIC WONDER FLUTE

UIGHUR

维吾尔

O nce upon a time, when wonder deeds were everyday deeds, there lived a Uighur in China's Sinkiang Province. He was rich in goods of the land, but not rich in kindness and goodness. Many people worked on his land and he had many cattle. But with all these riches he was mean and unkind to those around him. Most of all, he was mean to Anizu, a young shepherd lad who worked for him.

But Anizu was a happy fellow, worked hard, and found his greatest pleasure in playing the flute. His music was full of sweet magic, and all the people on the farm and in the village came to listen to his enchanting tunes. It also gave pleasure to the animals he tended. But there was one person who hated Anizu's music, and that was his master. The beautiful tunes filled him with black anger, and one day he became so enraged when he saw all his household listening to Anizu's playing that he tore the flute from the shepherd's hands, threw it on the ground, and stomped on it until it was smashed. With that, he told Anizu to leave and never show his face there again.

Anizu left with tears in his eyes and he walked along the road. Soon an old man came from the opposite direction. He stopped Anizu and said, "Why are you crying, young man? Whose boy are you? You have a golden life before you and should be happy."

"Alas! dear Grandfather! I was happy in my work as a shepherd. One of my joys was to play my flute, but this made my master very angry and he broke my flute to pieces and sent me from my work!"

"Young shepherd Anizu—you see, I know your name— do not worry about your flute and have no fear of finding work. I will make you the finest bamboo flute in Sinkiang, and you will earn much wealth with it. We will teach your mean master a lesson that will make a good man of him! Now I will make your new magic flute for you."

The old man cut off a thick hollow bamboo branch and shaped it into a flute. He tried a few notes on it and then gave it to Anizu. Anizu put it to his lips and began playing. Tunes came from it sweeter than the songs of the nightingale. People stopped to listen to the playing; beasts from the field came to hear the magic music of that magic flute! Nothing like it had ever been heard before!

Anizu's former master did not hear the magic music; he was always scolding and arguing.

One morning he rose very early and called his three sons to him.

"Sons," he said, "I had a strange dream last night. It was near sunset when suddenly there leaped up before me a little white rabbit with a spot of black hair on the top of its head. I want that white rabbit with the black fur on the top of its head. I never saw one like it. The one who brings it to me will get all I have."

And his three sons replied, "We have never heard of such a rabbit, let alone seen one. How are we to find it?"

"Nonsense!" said their father. "You have heard of it *now*. So go and look for it!"

The oldest of the three sons said, "Father, I am the oldest so it is my duty to do this for you and to gain your fortune. I will bring you the white rabbit with the black spot on the top of its head."

"Good," said the old father, "May luck go with you! Here is a bagful of money you will need on the way!"

The oldest son took the money, bade them all good-by, and went on the wide road.

He walked for a long time, when he saw an old man with a white beard coming toward him.

"Where to, young man, looking right and left?" asked the old man.

"I am looking for a little white rabbit with a black spot on its head. My old father wants it."

"If it is an animal you want, there is someone who can help. He is a shepherd who plays the flute. His hut is right at the end of the road."

The oldest son thanked the old man, walked on, and soon saw the hut.

When he saw Anizu he recognized him at once.

"Anizu," he said, "I am glad to see you again. My father dreamed of a white rabbit with black hair on its head. He wants that rabbit and I promised to find it for him. An old man I just met on the road said you could help me."

"I know that white rabbit and I remember you. If you will give me a thousand strings of coins from your bag I will get you the rabbit your father wants."

The oldest son gave him the strings of coins from his bag, and Anizu began to play his magic flute.

The music was sweeter than fresh honey, and very soon animals from the woods and birds from the air gathered around Anizu. The white rabbit with the black spot on its head came too. Quickly Anizu stopped and got hold of it by its long ears.

"Here is the rabbit, hold it tight, and bring it to your father. Don't let it escape."

The oldest son took hold of the rabbit and ran off quickly.

As soon as he was gone Anizu began playing on his magic flute. When the sweet tones reached the rabbit's long ears, it quickly wiggled out of the son's hands and was off faster than a falling star.

Sadly the oldest son came home and told his tale.

"Let me go," said the second son. "I promise you, dear Father, I will catch that rabbit and bring it to you."

The father gave him a bag of money, and the second son said good-by and went on the wide road.

The same thing happened to him as had happened to his brother.

He met the old man with the white beard, who sent him to Anizu. Anizu took his money, played the magic flute, caught the white rabbit, and gave it to the second son. Then he played the magic flute when the boy ran off with the rabbit, and the rabbit came back to Anizu. And—the second son came back empty-handed.

The father was very angry, but when the youngest son begged for a chance to bring the rabbit, the old father gave in, saying, "You *must* bring me the rabbit."

But the same happened to the youngest son as had happened to the other two, and he too came home without the rabbit.

The father was wild with anger. "Now I will show you three stupid fools what I can do. I will teach that fellow who takes the rabbit from you a lesson he will not forget."

The three sons were afraid to tell him it was Anizu, the young shepherd he had sent away, who had that white rabbit with the black spot on its head.

Anizu's former master ran off with a big stick in his hand.

He stomped along blindly. Anizu heard him coming, for he had been waiting for him. He put the magic flute to his lips and played the sweetest music heard in Sinkiang. Birds, animals, butterflies, snakes, and insects came from everywhere. Anizu pointed with his flute to the master, and all the creatures began flocking around him, plucking and pecking at him.

He recognized Anizu and was frightened to death and cried out, "Anizu! Anizu! Take the animals away from me! They will tear me apart! Stop your playing so that they leave me."

Anizu stopped playing for just a few moments.

"I will stop only if you swear you will give half of your wealth to those who work for you and to the poor."

"I promise! I swear!" the master cried. "Only take away the animals from me!"

Anizu stopped playing his magic flute, and the animals, one by one, returned to their own work and homes. Anizu and the master were soon alone.

"Anizu," said the master, "I am truly sorry for what I did and I promise I will share what I have with those who work for me and with those who need it."

"Then," said Anizu, "I will play my magic flute only to bring pleasure to all who will listen."

And so it was from then on.

# A MERRY PRANK OF PA-LENG-TS'ANG

MONGOL

蒙古

U p and down around the open steppes and sandy desert of Mongolia, on the north of vast China, Pa-leng-ts'ang traveled without end. Wherever he went he brought happy laughter, silver sayings, funny tricks, and wise thoughts. For that reason folks old and young, rich and poor, were happy to see him in their midst.

Once hot dusty day Pa-leng-ts'ang trundled along the road singing and dancing and thinking of a clever tale to tell in the next camp. Suddenly he saw coming toward him an important official and his followers on high horses. They recognized the famous trickster at once.

"Ha," said the official, "there goes that braggart Pa-leng-ts'ang, who thinks himself the cleverest fellow in all Mongolia! I'll show you how I can outtrick him and make a fool of him." He stopped his horse and shouted, "Ho there,

Pa-leng-ts'ang, you think you are the cleverest trickster in all our land. Well, show me you can get me off my horse if I do not want to get off!"

Pa-leng-ts'ang was silent for a while. Then, with a smile on his face, he said, "I agree with you. I cannot get you off your horse if you don't want to. But if you were standing on the ground, I could make you get on your horse whether you like it or not."

The stupid official leaped out of his saddle. "Show me," he cried. "Put me back on my horse!"

Pa-leng-ts'ang answered, "You see, I got you off your horse, didn't I?"

Now the official knew he had been tricked, so, grumbling, he climbed on his horse again to continue his trip. But Pa-leng-ts'ang laughed, "What do you say? Haven't I just made you get on your horse again, too? I have done both of the things you said I could not do!"

Everyone else laughed too as the official sheepishly rode off while Pa-leng-ts'ang walked on lightly, a smile on his face, thinking of the next merry prank.

# HUNTER HAILIBU'S GREAT SACRIFICE

MONGOL 蒙古

The Mongols who live in China and who are a part of the Chinese people tell a great tale of friendship, devotion, and sacrifice.

A crane flying high in the blue air spied a white snake sleeping on a stone. Swiftly she swooped down and caught the sleeping creature in her strong claws, turned upward, and began flying to her nest to make a meal out of the catch.

A Mongol hunter named Hailibu, out on his horse to find food, saw the crane and aimed with his bow and arrow. As the crane swerved suddenly, she loosened her claws, and the white snake fell and dropped on the grass, wriggling and alive.

The next morning Hailibu mounted his horse and set out, as he always did, to find food for the day. He had not ridden very far when he saw coming his way a group of snakes, among them the white snake whose life he had saved the day before.

They stopped his horse and greeted him in a very friendly way, and the white snake said, "You saved my life yesterday, and I have come with my friends to thank you. I am the daughter of a dragon king, and my parents asked me to invite you to their palace so that they can also thank you. When my father asks you what reward, what jewels you want for your good deed, don't ask for pearls or gold, but ask for the magic stone in his mouth. That magic stone is worth more than pearls or gold, for with it you will be able to understand the language of all living creatures, and that will be of great help all your life. But you must never tell anyone how you have that knowledge. If you do, you will turn into stone. Remember that."

"I will not forget your warning," Hailibu said.

Then the white snake and her escorts led him to the palace of the dragon king, deep down among the rocks.

The dragon king and his queen thanked Hailibu for having saved their child. Then the king said, "I want to reward you for your generous deed. Choose whatever you like from our treasures. Choose jewels and gold. I will give you anything you want."

"Your Majesty," said Hailibu, "I do not want jewels or gold. I ask only for the stone you hold in your mouth."

The king was silent for a time. Then he said, "I made a promise and I will keep it." With that, he opened his mouth and out fell a small stone that had been lying on the side. He gave it to Hailibu, who thanked him for it. Hailibu said good-by to those standing near him and was escorted out of the palace.

When he came home he soon knew what his horse said to the other horse, what the household animals said to one another, what all animals said. He found hunting much easier, for he learned from birds and beasts where there was good game. But he did not tell anyone how he had this knowledge, and soon he became the greatest hunter in all the land.

One day, resting next to his grazing horse, he saw and heard a large number of birds twittering wildly. He listened and understood what they were saying.

"Let us fly quickly from this place!" chirped the sparrow. "Yes, let us fly," cawed the crow. "Tomorrow the mountain will split apart! Wild waters will rush out and drown everyone and everything! We must fly! We must save ourselves. We must fly before the great flood comes!"

"Yes," said an owl in her deep voice, "the mountain will crack open. Waters will gush out and drown men and animals! Let's start right now! Tomorrow will be too late!"

The birds began flying off and Hailibu leaped on his horse and raced home. He was frightened and troubled and worried. "I, too, must fly, and my friends and relatives. I must warn everyone to flee, and I must tell them how I learned of this. I know that if I do, I will turn into stone, but I cannot see all these people drown. I must warn them, no matter what happens to me!"

He thought about this all night, and in the morning he decided he had to save the people. He rose early and began blowing on his horn. Men, women, and children soon were all there. Hailibu shouted, "Good friends, I know the language of the birds and I learned it when I saved the life of a white snake, the daughter of a dragon king. All the birds are flying and we all must do the same. The great mountain before us will split and giant streams of water will pour out and drown people and animals and destroy all that grows. Fly at once! Save yourselves. I will turn into stone for telling you this, but I must save you, no matter what happens to me."

As he was speaking, the sky became dark and there was rolling thunder and flashes of lightning.

All the people began running as fast as they could, but Hailibu stood still. He could not move.

There was a great crash of thunder, and lightning streaked the sky like wild birds. Then there was another terrific crash: the mountain burst apart and floods of water gushed forth.

The people had fled, but Hailibu could not move. His legs became cold and hard, and the same stoniness moved to the upper part of his body. Wild waves of water rushed around him, but he did not mind. He felt neither wet nor pain. Soon he felt nothing. . . . He was just a stone. . . .

For a time the winds and water, the thunder and lightning raged on, then slowly quieted. The waves and wind rolled Hailibu to the top of the mountain, and there he stopped.

The people came back and saw the great rock on the mountain. They knew it was Hailibu, who had given his life to save them. So they gave the rock his name and worshipped it for all he had done for them.

# THE
# TWINS OF
# PAIKALA
# MOUNTAIN

ORONCHON

鄂倫春

W eird doings happened in Paikala Mountain thousands of years ago. The mountain was a wonderful hunting ground, but few of the Oronchon ever hunted there. Why? Because in those hills there roamed a *mani*—a ferocious beast as tall as a tent and as ugly as an ape. He was ever on the lookout to eat anyone who dared to hunt on his mountain. His mouth stretched across his hairy face, ready to tear man and animal to pieces.

Nearby in the valley lived an elderly couple, unafraid and happy. They hunted and fished, never thinking of the *mani*. They went into the woods with their bows and arrows and brought down deer for food and tigers and leopards for skins to keep themselves warm.

In the fall the wife gave birth to twins, a boy and a girl. They were beautiful children and looked exactly alike.

169

The elder, a girl, they named Katuyen; the boy they called Altanay. Both grew up lovely as flowers; Katuyen became a fine worker in embroidery, and Altanay an unusually excellent archer.

When they were twelve years old a sad misfortune befell them. One day their parents went out to hunt and never returned. The *mani* had caught them! The children cried and cried and looked far and wide for their parents but could not find them. In their hearts they knew the *mani* had destroyed them.

Now they had to do the work their parents had done: they had to hunt for food and take care of each other. They went to work with a good will. Altanay hunted and fished and cut wood while Katuyen cured the hides, sewed, and cooked.

One evening when Altanay came home, Katuyen was not there. She had gone out to pick wild vegetables, leaving a kettle of boiling water on the fire. To while away the time, Altanay began sharpening his hunting knife. Suddenly there was a noise at the door and when he turned to see what it was —there stood a wild, fierce-looking creature with the head of an ape, roaring louder than six bears! It was the *mani*! Its wide-open mouth with long, sharp teeth was as big as its body, and the beast attacked Altanay . . . but he fought back with his hunting knife. They battled each other until Altanay stabbed the *mani* and killed it, but Altanay was so exhausted that he, too, fell down dead!

Soon Katuyen returned and saw the horrible sight of the dead *mani* and her dead brother. She tried everything to bring her brother back to life, but all her efforts were useless. Completely exhausted, she leaned against the giant pine tree outside the tent that was their home.

Remember that all this took place in the days when the spirits of trees and rocks talked to one another and to man as well.

Katuyen leaned against the pine tree, weeping over her

brother's fate, and the Spirit of the Pine felt sorry for her and said, "Take the yellow oil from me and put it all over the body of your brother. That will keep him until he can be brought back to life. Then send an archer to the great ocean where Salgutai rules. He has three daughters who may be able to bring your brother back to life. But the archer you send must be so skilled that he can shoot a whole flock of geese with a single arrow."

"Where can I find an archer who can shoot a flock of geese with a single arrow!" Katuyen thought. But she had courage and determination. She put on her brother's clothes, tucked her black hair under his hunting cap, and flung his bow and arrow over her back. At that the Spirit of the Pine shook off a strong bough that turned into a fine horse, which she mounted, armed and ready to set off to Salgutai. On the horse Katuyen practiced shooting arrows from the bow. First she brought down one bird, then two, then three. Day by day, with practice, she became better with her bow and arrow. Soon she could bring down sixteen geese with one arrow.

On and on the magic horse kept galloping, and one sun-filled hour there was the blue ocean before her. When the horse neighed, two wings grew on its sides, and both horse and rider skimmed swiftly over the dancing white waves to the island where Salgutai ruled.

The horse and rider were welcomed by the three daughters of the chieftain, and it did not take long before all three fell in love with the beautiful young visitor. The chieftain did not want to see any of his daughters leave him, so he planned to rid himself of the guest. He ordered a great feast to be set on the stone tables under the green-leaved trees. There were many kinds of food, fruits, and drinks. But Katuyen was suspicious and ate and drank only the food and wine that Salgutai ate and drank. Salgutai watched her and became angry. For nine days the feast went on, and Salgutai's patience ran out.

"For nine days you have tried to outwit me," the chieftain shouted. "Now you will have only one choice. I shall wink my eyes five times, then you must drink up one of the crocks of wine before you. If you don't, your head will go rolling with the wind."

No sooner was Salgutai's head turned than his daughters signaled to Katuyen to drink only the red wine and not to touch the yellow. Katuyen drank up the whole crock of red wine and cried out, "Now I want to sleep." She stumbled away from the table, running toward the sea, and fell down on the beach pretending to sleep.

As the sun went down, Salgutai sent his soldiers with lighted torches to bring Katuyen back, for he was determined to destroy her. Katuyen saw them approach and knew full well why they were coming. When they came near enough she raised her bow, inserted an arrow, and with a single shot cut off ninety-nine of their torches. This frightened the soldiers so much that they ran back to their chieftain to tell him of the powerful strength of the young "man."

Then Salgutai called his three daughters and said to them, "Here, take this magic hairpin, an ancient heirloom in our family, and follow the young hunter to his home. Use the hairpin at the right moment, which you will know when it comes. Also take these magic goose feathers. If any of you wants to come back, just put one of the feathers in your hair and you will turn into a goose and you can then fly home."

The three girls came to Katuyen with their magic gifts and said, "We will come with you." Katuyen put them behind her on her magic horse and soon they zoomed through the air to Katuyen's home in the Paikala Mountain of the Greater Khingan Range.

She saw her tent and brought the horse down before it.

Then Katuyen said to the three sisters, "You wait here while I go into the tent to make everything ready for you. Then I will call you."

In the tent there was her brother, still lying well-preserved by the magic pine oil. She quickly put on her own clothes, let down her lovely black hair, and went behind a tiger's skin that was hanging there. Then she shouted for the three sisters to come in.

The three entered and stopped in great surprise before the dead Altanay, who looked exactly like Katuyen.

They said to one another, "How quickly he has fallen asleep!" They tried to wake him, but he remained stiff and cold. The eldest cried, "This is a trick I cannot understand."

Said the second, "Let us go home quickly or we will be blamed for his death."

But the youngest said, "Let us use our silver magic hairpin with which life can be brought back."

The two elder sisters fought to be the first to use the hairpin, for the three agreed that whoever brought the young man back to life would marry him. The youngest sister generously suggested following the custom of letting the eldest start. So the eldest sister took the silver hairpin and drew a circle around Altanay, but he did not move. The second did the same, but Altanay did not move. "Come," she cried, "come, let us fly home. I don't think it is good for us to stay here."

"You are right," said the eldest.

They left the magic hairpin to the youngest, then put the magic goose feathers in their hair, turned into a pair of geese, and flew off.

The youngest sister took the magic silver hairpin and first stuck it into the earth near where Altanay lay. His chest began to move. Then she drew a circle around him with the magic pin. Altanay sat up, looked around him bewildered, stared at the girl's face, and said, "Who are you? What has happened?"

The girl was too astonished to answer, but right then Katuyen came from behind the tiger skin and said, "My brother is alive again, thanks to your magic power! You were in love with me, but I am a woman, too. My brother is like me. Why not marry him—a man?"

The two were married and they lived with Katuyen happily ever after.

KOREAN 朝鮮

# THE CHOOSY MAID OF YEN-PIEN

KOREAN 朝鮮

I n ancient China, there lived in what is present-day Yen-pien a Korean maiden whom all people envied and admired. She could work better and more quickly than anyone in the land. She could fry a mess of beans by a streak of lightning. In fact, she could fry three messes of beans while one flash flashed across the sky!

In a morning she could steam her raw hemp, separate the fibers, spin them into thread, and weave the threads into linen finer than the finest silk. So swiftly did her fingers work that she still had time to cook rice, put it in a wooden box, cover it with the cloth she had woven, and carry it all for breakfast to the men working in the fields. She was famous throughout the land for thousands of *li*, and many a young man tried to marry her. The matchmakers almost wore out the doorsill of her front door, but she would have none of the suitors.

One day a fine young man from a faraway village came to woo her. He said he could work as well as she could. He could plant ten *mou*\* of rice in a single morning.

"I would like to see you do it."

"I will come tomorrow and you will see."

The next morning, just as the gleaming sun rose, he was there and began planting the seedlings without stopping.

On and on he worked, and when the sun had climbed to the center of the sky, before the dew on the grass was even dry, he had planted ten *mou*, just as he said he would.

When the maiden came to inspect the field, the young man turned around to look for his straw hat. He was so set on his work that he had forgotten he had put it down in the rice paddy.

The maiden looked at him and smiled.

"You are a good worker," she said, "but you left out this spot that was covered by your hat. Your work is still not good enough for me, and I will not marry you."

The poor disappointed young man left in a huff.

Not long after, another young man arrived, handsome and strong, to woo the maiden. He, too, said he could plant ten *mou* of rice in just half a day.

Again she said, "I would like to see you do it."

"I will tomorrow."

The morrow came and so did the young man. He began working, planting, working.

The sun reached the middle of the sky and ten *mou* were planted.

The maiden came and examined the work.

"Yes, I see ten *mou* of rice seedlings planted, but I also see one unplanted seedling floating on the water."

"Yes," said the young man, "I forgot one of the seedlings."

\* A *mou* is about one-sixth of an acre.

"Young man," she said, "you forgot one of the seedlings, and that means your work is not good enough. I will not marry you."

After that the Korean young men of China were afraid to ask for the maiden and none came.

Life for her at home became lonely, and so she decided to go out into the land to see if she could find the right man for her. She roamed about for some time, and one day, while crossing the top of a mountain, she met one of the young men she had refused. He was still angry, and when she came face to face with him on the narrow path, he pushed her off the cliff on which she was standing.

At that moment a young blacksmith in the village below was hammering out a scythe. Seeing the falling girl, he finished the scythe and dashed out to the foot of the mountain. Quicker than a flash of lightning he cut off a mess of twigs, wove them into a basket, and held it under the falling maiden. She fell right in without a scratch.

She jumped out of the basket and cried, "You saved my life!"

He was big and strong and manly. She looked at him and cried, "Perhaps you are the man for whom I have been looking!"

He recognized who she was—the outstanding maiden in all the northeast.

"You will make a fine wife," he said.

"And I think you will make a fine husband."

So they were married and were happy ever after.

# THE COMPETITIVE TIGER

KAWA

Tigers are big, strong creatures. They are almost as strong as roaring lions and often just as fierce and fearless. They growl when they are angry, but you know the biggest noises come from the largest hollow drums.

One day a big heavy tiger was stalking along the woods. He was strong and proud and believed himself to be the most powerful creature in all Yunnan. Soon he came to some vines laden with bean pods, dangling from a tree. Among the perfumed branches of the tree was a little yellow bird dancing from twig to twig and from vine to vine, twittering a little song all the time.

Tiger stopped and watched him for a while. Then he said, "Poor little bird, why this singing and dancing? Is it a holiday? Look at me, I am a thousand times bigger and stronger than you are. I don't go around hopping and dancing and singing. Why do you?"

"Noble Tiger, I cannot bellow like you, but with all your size and strength, I'll bet you cannot dance as I do from twig to twig and from vine to vine."

"Ho! ho! ho!" growled Tiger. "I can do anything you do and do it better. I'll show you *right now!*" And, saying this, he leaped onto the vine, tearing and breaking branches and showering bean pods all over. In the end, he fell down on the rocks on the ground, cutting and bruising himself.

The little yellow bird twittered loudly, dancing on the vines that were left. "Who wins? Who wins?" he twittered.

Tiger only growled, got up from the ground and limped off, angry and in pain.

He limped through the woods until he came to a sunny open field. There he saw a sight that made him forget his pain and anger.

In the middle of the field lay a small animal, all fur and no legs!

Tiger thought this funny and began to laugh. It was a young mole, taking a nap.

"What are you laughing at?" said the mole in a piping voice.

"At you. At you, you funny little creature with no ears, no feet, no legs. Ho! ho!, and no eyes either! Ho! ho! ho! What are you?"

Mole was angry and insulted.

"So I have no eyes and no feet! No feet like you! Heavy tree-trunk feet! I wouldn't boast about them. See that crowd of people working in the field? I'll bet you I can run through that crowd with my little feet quicker than you can with your great big tree trunks."

"Ho! ho! ho!" bellowed Tiger, "let us see."

Mole got up on his little feet and scuttled across the field to the crowd of workers. They took off their turbans, which they used to try to catch him, but he dodged quickly and soon ran through the crowd.

"Now, Tiger, you go," he piped.

Tiger took a great leap into the crowd, but when they saw him coming, they raised their clubs and crossbows, anything on which they could lay their hands, and beat Tiger until he had to run to save his life.

He ran and Mole ran with him until they were both too tired to run any more.

Mole lay down and stretched out his feet.

"What are these?" asked Tiger, panting, "what are these twig-looking things hanging from you?"

"These are my feet that look like twigs to you but which beat your tree-trunk feet," answered Mole. "I will keep my little feet and you can keep your noisy bumpers."

Tiger did not like this and he made ready to leap on Mole to tear him to pieces, but Mole quickly slipped into his hole and Tiger was left standing foolishly before the hole.

Tiger limped away tired and in pain and came to a round swampy hole filled with black earth and brown leaves.

He lapped up and drank some water and lay down at the rim. A snail was slowly twisting across the top of the swampy hole.

Forgetting the lesson he should have learned from the bird and the mole, he began to laugh, watching the little snail wriggling slowly, very slowly.

"Ho! ho! ho! What an ugly little thing—no mouth! no legs! What can you do?"

"You may be big in size," Snail answered. "You can leap and I can only crawl, yet I would bet you that I can get across this swamp more quickly with my crawling than you can with your leaping."

Tiger laughed until tears ran from his eyes. "Ho! ho! ho!"

"You begin your crawling, and when you are halfway across, I will be on the other side with one leap."

"Talking and doing are as far apart as Heaven and Earth," said Snail, wriggling on.

Tiger sat on the edge of the swamp laughing. Then, after a time he got up, crouched on his hind legs, and took a strong leap over the swamp. But alas! Tiger was heavy and a little tired from the morning's adventures, so he misjudged the distance and his strength and—he fell right in the middle of the swamp.

He began pushing and tugging, trying to get up and out. But the more he pushed and tugged, the deeper he sank, while Snail was wriggling on and on toward the other side.

Tiger heaved and tried to leap up, but only sank back deeper. Soon only his head was seen above the black swamp.

Snail reached the other side and wriggled around to look for Tiger.

But alas! There was no Tiger anywhere! There were only a few bubbles on the black swampy water!

APPENDICES

# NOTES

## THE CHAO KU BIRD (Han)

"*Chao*" means "to search," "*ku*" is the name for a sister-in-law, specifically the sister of one's husband. The Chinese have a name for each kind of relative, so that when a person addresses another member of the family, you can tell instantly whether he or she is talking to an older or younger person, a sibling or a cousin, a paternal or maternal relative, or uncle or aunt who is older or younger than one's parent, if the relationship is by blood or by marriage, etc.

The *chao ku* bird is so named because of its cry. This name is a folk name based on the story of the lost sister-in-law. The bird is possibly a cuckoo, which is called *chu jiu* or *pu ku*; if one juxtaposes the two names, one gets *chu ku*, which is quite close to *chao ku*. It might also be the common partridge, which is called *che ku* in Chinese. Judging by the cry attributed to the *chao ku* bird, we favor the cuckoo as a choice.

In old China, when a girl married, she was considered a member of her husband's family forever.


## THE GREAT DEEDS OF KING YÜ (Han)

King Yü is often called Ta Yü or Yü the Great. He was said to have been minister to King Yao and later to King Shun, who succeeded Yao. In turn Yü succeeded Shun and founded the Hsia dynasty, which then became hereditary. Together with Yao and Shun, Yü is worshipped by the Taoists as one of the San Kuan, or Three Rulers, who preside over Heaven, earth, and water.

Yü is best known for directing the waters of China. According to records that are not historical, he spent nine years draining the great floods. The Chinese seem to have a deep memory for these floods. In this respect, they are like the Westerners who believe in Noah and the Deluge. Although the Hsia dynasty was recorded as real, its existence has not yet been proven, but with excavations going on all over China and new discoveries being made, archaeological evidences are beginning to emerge. We may yet find that King Yü was a historical figure. In this story from Shantung Province, he is described as a folk hero, which could be close to the truth.

Most of the main rivers in China proper flow from the west to the east. This story tries to explain how they came to be that way.


## THE TALE OF THE SHRIMP AND
## THE EARTHWORM (Han)

The pronunciation for the word "shrimp" is "hsia" in Chinese. The pronunciation for the word "blind" is also "hsia"; therefore this tale about a shrimp who was blind is based upon a pun. The Chinese language is full of "homophones"—words that sound alike

—so punning is a great national sport. Many jokes, aphorisms, and stories are built on puns.

## THE MAGIC BOAT (Han)

A eunuch was a castrated male who lived in the palace and served the emperor's family. He was allowed to be near the women of the royal clan as other men were not, and he often became very powerful because of his influence over them. Chinese history tells of many eunuchs who were involved in intrigue and politics, sometimes rising to positions of great power and wealth and sometimes even causing the fall of dynasties. There were eunuchs in Chinese courts until the revolution of 1911.

A "flower chair" is a sedan chair borne on poles on the shoulders of chair carriers. It is covered with embroidered materials, which give it this name. Chinese brides were taken to their weddings in these covered chairs from ancient times well into the 20th century.

## THE SAD TALE OF THE RABBIT'S TAIL (Han)

In old China, a large family was very much prized. Today, the Chinese population is estimated at over 950 million. Nearly one-fourth of the people of the world live in the People's Republic of China. In new China, the people are being encouraged to have smaller families, so that there will be enough housing and food for all. Rabbit and Turtle would not boast of their large families today!

## A TRUE MONEY TREE (Han)

This story comes from Shantung Province, the home of the sage Confucius. It illustrates well the Confucian teaching of respect for one's parents.

This story also illustrates the Chinese work ethic. In order to feed and clothe the vast population of China, every man, woman, and child must work very hard.

## THE RED STREAM (Han)

In old China a daughter-in-law's duty was to serve her parents-in-law and husband. A son was supposed to put the welfare of his father and mother above that of his wife or children. Even a stepmother carried the same authority as a real mother, and she had the right to order about her stepson's wife. A son could not criticize his parents for their treatment of his wife. This system worked when the older people were kind and understanding, but it caused much unhappiness when they were cruel or unreasonable. Many stories are told about such unhappy situations.

That Yü Hua and Shih Tun lived happily with the kind old woman proved that they were good young people, even though they had run away from his stepmother. They respected old people and were willing to serve and help them.

The Chinese believed that all aspects of nature—such as trees, flowers, rocks, etc.—had spirits of their own, and that sometimes they turned into monsters, sometimes into benign fairies. Very old trees or old animals especially were likely to be spirits.

The name Yü Hua means "Jade Flower." The name Shih Tun means "Stone Bin"; it refers to a stone bin in which grains are stored. "Stone Bin" as a name calls forth the image of someone who is very sturdy and solid, a reservoir of strength.

## THE TALE OF THE GOLDEN VASE
## AND THE BRIGHT MONKEYS (Tibetan)

The *jen-shen kuo*, translated literally as the "jen-shen fruit," is a plant with an edible root, which is starchy and sweet. Its Latin name is *Pontilla anseria L.* The common name *"jen-shen"* is exactly the same as "ginseng" in Chinese, and therefore easily confused. The Latin name for "ginseng" is *Panax schin-seng Nees*, and it is a medicinal plant.


# THE BIRD OF HAPPINESS (Tibetan)

In this story, when the Bird of Happiness gives "butter-cakes" to Wang-ga to eat, presumably it is referring to yak butter, of which the Tibetans are very fond. They even put yak butter in their tea.


# THE TIBETAN ENVOY'S MISSION
(Tibetan)

This story comes from the Eastern Tibetans who live in Szechuan, the province just east of Tibet. These people are obviously proud of being Tibetans and relish this tale of their clever envoy, but like many folks who tell stories of happenings of long ago, they make mistakes about historical facts. It is true that Emperor T'ai-tsung married Princess Wen-ch'eng to the King of Tibet, but she was not his daughter; she was a kinswoman. It is true that the King of Tibet sent an envoy to the T'ang court, but the trials were made up by storytellers. A very famous painter of the T'ang dynasty named Yen Li-pen (died 673 A.D.) painted a picture of Emperor T'ai-tsung receiving the Tibetan envoy. This painting belongs to the Palace Museum in Peking, and the upper part of our illustration is an adaptation of it. The lower part, or foreground, of our illustration is adapted from a mural in the tomb of a T'ang princess, the Princess Yung-t'ai.

The T'ang dynasty lasted from 618 to 907 A.D. It is known as China's Golden Age, and the greatest emperor of that period was

T'ai-tsung. His title means "Great Lord." T'ai-tsung cared a great deal about the welfare of his people and valued their opinion of him. He appointed good officials and promoted art and literature. During his reign, the design of the Chinese civil-service examination system was completed; it lasted more than a thousand years, until the revolution of 1911. T'ai-tsung welcomed foreigners and treated them as equals, partly because his family had foreign blood through marriage. In 630 A.D. he crushed the nomadic Eastern Turks who had been plaguing the Chinese in the north. His prestige rose so high that many tribes sent envoys to ask for T'ang protection. They presented him with the title of "Heavenly Khan" or the "Khan of Khans." China became the leader of an alliance made up of kingdoms in East, Central, and South Asia, even at times including India and Persia.

The name Wen-ch'eng may be translated as "Accomplished in the Arts," for "Wen" means "literature," or, more broadly, "the arts"; Ch'eng means "accomplished." Emperor T'ai-tsung married his kinswoman Princess Wen-ch'eng to the first King of Tibet after he repelled an invasion by Tibet in 641. It was his way of pacifying a former foe. The princess brought to Tibet Chinese culture as well as the Buddhist religion.

Because the T'ang court was so cosmopolitan, the capital Ch'ang-an was the gathering place of visitors and tradespeople from a number of different nations. Many came by caravans, often bringing horses to sell. T'ang people valued these imported steeds as people value their fancy cars today, so we can understand why this tale, in part, concerns horses. Because China was then a leader among nations, the T'ang court received many gifts, or tributes, from foreign lands. This tale refers to the hair lotion from a faraway country that the princess received as a gift.

Today we see clay figures of T'ang horses and camels, as well as of people: court ladies, soldiers, officials, foreign merchants, grooms, and camel herds—an endless variety—in museums all over the world. These are "tomb figurines" that were buried with the dead; they were supposed to accompany the departed soul and serve him or her in the other world. In America, the Art Institute of Chicago, the Nelson Gallery in Kansas City, and Royal Ontario Museum of Toronto, among others, have rich collections of T'ang figurines.

# BIG BROTHER—MAN; LITTLE BROTHER—RABBIT (Ch'iang)

This story reminds one of the tale of *Br'er Rabbit and the Tar Baby* in the way the rabbit was caught.

The story tells us that the mother and son planted *hu-tou* and *yuan-ken*. *Tou* could be either peas or beans in Chinese, but the mention of discarded pods favors the translation "peas." *Hu-tou* means literally "foreign peas (or beans)." *Yuan-ken* means "round roots," which could be potatoes or some other root vegetable such as carrots. The story mentions the sweet taste of the vegetable as well as discarded skins, so we have used the translation "yams." This kind of translation problem can be solved only by a visit to the actual locality, since the names used are peasant terms, not botanical.

Sugar and lard are luxury items in the diet of countryfolk. The sugar- and lard-centered steamed buns mentioned here are made by using cubes of lard mixed with sugar or rock candy as centers inside yeast-raised flour dough. The buns are steamed, making the lard and sugar melt. Sometimes these are called "Crystal buns," because the lard turns transparent under heat.

Each locality is believed to be governed by a Soil God or Earth God. He is a sort of supernatural magistrate, and the people pray to him for blessings and protection.

# A WELL-DESERVED PUNISHMENT (Yi)

The Chinese people believe that anyone who commits a wrong, especially against his parents, friends, ruler, or some defenseless person, may be punished by a thunderbolt from Heaven. To die from being struck by lightning almost automatically stigmatizes the victim. In this tale Rock Pigeon chides her friend for not helping and hints that Heaven may send a thunderbolt to hit him. Her remarks are a reflection of the Yi people's sense of justice and the importance they attach to hard work and co-operation among friends.

# THE WINDING-HORN VILLAGE (Pai)

This story appears in the unofficial history of the Kingdom of Nan-chao, founded around 740 A.D. in Yunnan Province. Western sinologists believe the people of Nan-chao were the Tai, who later moved south to found modern Siam (Thailand), but Chinese scholarship identifies them as Lolo. This story was supposedly about the daughter of the Nan-chao king named Kolofeng. However, a folktale with fuller details was developed later, supposedly about the daughter of the Pai king. The Pai, originally called Min-chia, is a Tibeto-Burman people who conquered the Kingdom of Nan-chao and established the Kingdom of Tali in Yunnan. They are a separate group from the Tai and the Lolo. Our tale is the Pai version.

Pai means "white" in Chinese; therefore the Pai king's son is called "White Forest" and his daughters are "White Crane" and "White Jade."

Apparently there is a local mountain called Blue Mountain and a rock at the foot of it that is called "Beauty Rock."

Lake Erh Hai is a famous large lake near the city of Tali in Yunnan Province. The ancient kingdom of Nan-chao also had Tali as its capital.

The village is named Winding-Horn Village because the water buffalo turned and twisted its horns to get through the narrow alleys to reach the old woman's house.

The young women hid themselves when the prince went among the common people to search for a wife probably because the common people felt it was dangerous to associate with royalty and were afraid.

# T'IEN THE BRAVE, HERO OF THE HSIA RIVER (Tuchia)

The Hero of super-human strength is a favorite of folk tales. T'ien the Brave reminds us of Paul Bunyan, although the Tuchia people do not emphasize his size so much as his physical power, mental agility, and kindness of heart. They consider him one of their ancestors and a pioneer who enabled them to settle Hunan Province as well as the Western part of Hupei Province.

Hunan Province is dominated by a huge basin into which several rivers flow to form the famous Tung-t'ing Lake. The Hsia River is probably a tributary of one of them. As the waters that leave Tung-t'ing Lake eventually join the Yangtze, which divides China into North and South, all these rivers may be said to belong to the Yangtze River system. The lake is full of silt and the rivers are prone to turbulent flooding during summers and autumns—a very likely explanation for the ending of this tale, when the Hsia River rose and inundated the wharf and inn, killing T'ien's enemies.

## WHY THE SUN RISES
## WHEN THE ROOSTER CROWS (Hani)

This story is similar to the Han tale of *Erh-lang and the Suns*, but it has a different twist and ending.

The rooster appears in folk tales of many nations and is often associated with the sunrise.

A winnowing basket is used to separate the chaff from the grain. It resembles a dust pan with no handles. Holding this pan with both hands, the farmer tosses the grain into the air, causing the lighter chaff to fly away as the heavier grain falls back into the basket.

## THE HEAVENLY SONG OF THE
## GREEN-SPOTTED DOVE (Lisu)

This story is a reflection of the Lisu people's love for music and the inspiration they derive from Nature, for they tell many stories in songs and even settle their disputes with songs. It is also interesting to find in this tale the theme of falling into a cave to find oneself in another world. We are reminded of *Alice in Wonderland*, which is not a folk tale but written by a sophisticated author, Lewis Carroll. Apparently the native intelligence and imagination of the Lisu people are just as keen and lively.

## THE WHITE-HAIR WATERFALL (Tung)

A Chinese red radish is usually larger than the ones in America. It is longer and thicker, shaped more like a carrot; therefore it is easy to imagine its being used as a plug for stopping up a hole.

## THE STORY OF THE HOUSE (Shui)

The Shui people have a drinking song based upon this story. It goes something like this:

That is yours!
This is mine!
The first fire
Singed the Dragon's scales;
The first flame
Striped the Tiger's skin.
The frightened Dragon hid in the sea,
The dashing Tiger howled into the hills,
Twisting around one turn after another,
Leaping over one rock after another.
Why won't you linger, my friend?
Why are you seen no more, my friend?

## THE TALE OF THE MAGIC
## GREEN WATER-PEARL (Nung)

The firepit around which the villagers sat to keep warm was made of stones. Over the fire, the people put a three-legged cooking pot in which they cooked rice.

Yen-kang called his neighbor Uncle Lu. It is a common practice in China to call older folks "Uncle" or "Aunt" even if they are not related to you. This form of address shows respect and affection.

Uncle Lu mentioned a shaman. A shaman is a witch-priest who tells fortunes and performs magic. He is very much like the "medicine man" in Indian tribes.

## THE WONDERFUL CHUANG BROCADE
(Chuang)

Many Chinese people believe in reincarnation. They believe that good people will be rewarded in the next life and those who are bad will be punished. A cruel or greedy person may come back as an animal or even an insect. A kind and honest person may return as a rich man. So Letui was hoping that their next life would be better than that of poor woodcutters.

## THE GOD OF FACES (Tai)

This story mentions the Salween River, which flows from southwest China through east Burma to the Bay of Bengal, therefore establishing the origin of the tale near the Burma-China border.

The sprinkling of water is a Tai practice during ceremonies of offering to the gods. Water is sprinkled from vessels to the ground as a symbol of devotion. The Tai also celebrate a Water Sprinkling Festival that has a legendary origin (see description of the Tai minority).

All Buddhists believe in reincarnation. In this story, the Tai people tell us how each soul coming to the earth acquires a new face for his lifetime.

## THE PEACOCK'S TAIL (Miao)

This story comes from the Miao people of Kweichow Province. The saying about this area is "There is no level ground for three *li*, and there is no sunny sky for over three days." Kweichow is hilly and rainy, and most of the Miao people live in the forests and mountains. The weather, however, is relatively mild. From this story, we can deduce what kind of animals the Miao people are familiar with.

## SMART HEAD BETTER THAN SHARP TEETH (Kazakh)

The Kazakhs are nomadic shepherds who in the summer live in felt-covered tents called *yurts*. In the winter they live in mud and wood houses.

Kazakhs also track animals on horseback. In this story the hunter sets a trap. The animals they try to catch are wolves and foxes whose furs are valuable.

## A MERRY PRANK OF PA-LENG-TS'ANG (Mongol)

This story comes from a collection of Mongolian humorous tales, the central character of which is Pa-leng-ts'ang. He is such a well-known personality that his very name is synonymous with merriment. To the Mongols, Pa-leng-ts'ang is the "King of Humor."

## HUNTER HAILIBU'S GREAT SACRIFICE (Mongol)

We usually think of Mongols as nomads living in tents on grassy plains. They move their temporary settlements from place to place to find the best grazing grounds. If we look at the map of China, however, we find that there are also tall mountains in Inner Mongolia near the bend of the Yellow River. Many Mongols also live in Western Manchuria, where there are high mountains. We do not know exactly from which part of China this Mongol tale came, but it must have come from a tribe that hunted near some mountain range.

## THE TWINS OF PAIKALA MOUNTAIN
(Oronchon)

This story describes very well the dangerous and hard life of Oronchon hunters and tells us something about the qualities they admire—bravery and perseverance, loyalty and devotion, skill in shooting and riding. Its theme of a woman in masculine disguise surpassing men in martial feats is a familiar one in the tales of other nations, but this version has a romantic twist, and the savagery of the story, rooted in the Oronchon's sense of mystery of the forest, is tempered by poetic touches such as the image of the two sisters flying home as a pair of geese.

## THE CHOOSY MAID OF YEN-PIEN (Korean)

This story comes from the Yen-pien Korean Autonomous District, which is in the eastern part of Kirin Province, bordering North Korea.

We are not sure whether the fiber used for weaving the linen cloth is ramie or hemp. The reference to the silken quality of the fabric would seem to indicate ramie, but hemp is commonly planted in Kirin; it is therefore a more likely choice. Both ramie and hemp are called "*ma*" in Chinese, and both are used to produce linen cloth.

This story has a sequel:

After their marriage the two young persons had six sons, and since the parents were wonderful people, the sons were unusual children. Each son had a magic gift. The eldest could foretell fortunes. The second could open all locks. The third could not be chopped down even with an ax. The fourth was unhurt by fire. The fifth could not be drowned. The sixth could not be crushed by any weight.

One day their father the blacksmith had a violent dispute with a corrupt official who became his fierce enemy. The corrupt official jailed the blacksmith, but he was rescued by his sons. Then the villain tried every kind of punishment to destroy the blacksmith—drowning, burning, crushing, and other horrible torments. Each time a son thwarted the corrupt official. In the end the official gave up trying, for he saw he could not win. He shut his eyes and said, "I don't see that blacksmith, so he must be dead!"

# NOTES
## ABOUT THE ETHNIC GROUPS

## THE HAN MAJORITY

In the Introduction to this book, we tried to call attention to the different types of Han people who make up the majority of the Chinese population. Now we shall try to explain what they have in common.

Almost all the Han or "ethnic" Chinese live in the eastern part of the country, which has more rainfall and less rugged terrain than does the rest of China, and is therefore better suited to agriculture. The area the Han occupy takes up about 46 percent of the total land of China and is traditionally divided into the central plains, the north, the northeast, the south and the southwest.

Different dialects are spoken in various parts of China, but they are essentially variants of the same language; and since roughly 70 percent of the Han people speak some form of *p'u-t'ung-hua*—Mandarin—it has been adopted as the national dialect.

Furthermore, from the second millenium B.C., when the earliest-known writing was recorded on bones, all the ethnic Chinese have used the same system, which consists of pictographs (picture writing) and ideographs (idea writing) as well as characters that are combinations with one part representing pictures or ideas and another part representing sounds, but the system is not phonetic. Instead of reading words by spelling, the reader recognizes them by strokes; therefore the writing is understandable to people from different areas where pronunciations are not the same. This common written language is the strongest bond among Han people.

Besides language, the Han people share a history that dates back about 4000 years. Their civilization originated in the central plains of the Yellow River and spread southeastward, southwestward, and northeastward. Thus from about 3000 years ago they called their nation the "Central Kingdom" and themselves "People of the Central Kingdom." All Chinese recognize this history as the story of their people; they also call themselves "Han," because the Han dynasty (202 B.C.—220 A.D.) was the first durable unified empire under which they established themselves as political and cultural leaders in East Asia.

With the same language and history, the Han Chinese naturally share a common culture. Until the present time about 80 percent of them lived in rural areas. For centuries their livelihood was tied to the land and geared to the lunar calendar, although crops differed according to climate and soil. The other 20 percent of Han people lived in cities and were merchants, industrial workers, craftsmen, and administrators; for the cities served from the beginning of history as the seats of governments as well as centers for commerce, learning, the arts and gracious living. Today the People's Republic of China is trying to give the rural population more autonomy and bring their living standards closer to the level of urban residents.

One of the dominant features of Chinese culture was the "clan," in which relatives banded together and helped one another. The family was so important that each person was expected to put its interest above his own. On the positive side, individuals enjoyed a sense of belonging and a kind of "social security" in times of need; but the system also tended to encourage nepotism and corruption, perpetuate wealth and power in relatively few big families and coddle their idle and non-productive members. Today the Communist government discourages the concept of "clan." In many places *communes* have been established as social and economic units and their members are learning to live and produce in teams. The nuclear family is becoming more important in China as well as with the Chinese emigrants in industrialized nations, where individual achievement counts more than does family prominence.

As China becomes a modern nation, undoubtedly more changes will take place, but the Han people will always be bound by their common language and heritage. Their sense of identity is so strong that no matter where he lives, every Chinese refers to himself as a "person of the Central Kingdom" or "Han."

## MINORITY NATIONALITIES
## REPRESENTED BY STORIES IN THIS BOOK

### THE CH'IANG

The Ch'iang were mentioned in the earliest records of Chinese history. After the collapse of the Han dynasty (202 B.C.–220 A.D.) China was briefly divided into three warring kingdoms that were later reunified in 280 A.D. The new emperor then made the mistake of admitting foreigners for the purpose of replenishing the greatly reduced population. This ushered in almost three hundred years of chaos, when barbarians overran the Central Kingdom, bringing a profound cultural and racial mix. The Ch'iang are remembered as one of the "Five Barbarians" who dominated the scene at that time.

Today the Ch'iang are estimated to be between 40,000 and 50,000, living, for the most part, in northwest Szechuan Province, Kansu and Ch'inghai. In Szechuan they are concentrated on the two banks of the Min River, flanked by the Min Mountains, whose lofty peaks and dense forests are the storehouses of various animals, plants, and insects from which medicines and perfumes are made, including the much treasured musk. Here also is the home of the panda and the golden-haired monkey.

The early Ch'iang barbarians are thought by Western scholars to be northern Tibetans or Tanguts. Their descendants speak a language belonging to the Tibeto-Burman branch of the Sino-Tibetan family, but most of them also know how to speak and write Chinese. Now an agricultural people, they live in villages of mud and stone houses the architecture of which resembles that of Tibetan dwellings. These homes vary in the number of stories, the lowest reserved for animals. Their flat roofs are connected by wooden boards over which neighbors can walk and visit one another.

The Ch'iang are monogamous. They believe in many gods and have deities for the sky, the sun, the earth, and the mountains, as well as for animals such as sheep or for trades such as iron-smithing or stonecutting. Each village has at least one shaman who conducts religious rituals for weddings and funerals and exorcises evils that cause illnesses. Ch'iang temples for dragon gods or Taoist deities are very similar to those of the Han.

## THE CHUANG

The Chuang people are the largest minority of China. Estimated to number 8 to 10 million, they live mostly in the Kwangsi Chuang Autonomous Region, taking up about ⅓ the total population of Kwangsi Province. Some are also scattered in neighboring provinces. The Chuang are so well assimilated that it is difficult to distinguish them from the Han, but they have their own spoken language. Since they had no written language, the Chinese government helped to create a writing system in 1954 so that they could receive formal education.

Chuang settlements are usually near the water, and their houses are built on piles or stilts. Most of the people are farmers whose methods are very similar to those of the Han; they plant rice in paddies and use water buffalo for plowing.

The Chuang are organized into clans. Marriage is arranged

through a matchmaker, and the bride stays with her parents until a child is born. Then she goes to live with her husband. In the past, a man often had several wives.

Very little is recorded about Chuang religion, but we know that Chuang people believe in magic and spirits and that their magicians practice sorcery using doll images.

Chuang culture dates back to ancient days; 2000 years ago their ancestors already knew how to make bronze drums. Their weaving of brocade is famous, and they maintain a high standard in drawing and painting. To this day in the southwest of Kwangsi Province on the Flower Mountain Range (Hua Shan) along the Ming River (Ming Chiang), huge murals are preserved.

Singing is a favorite pastime of the Chuang people. Individuals are skillful in making up their own songs, and group singing is part of celebrations. During a courting festival, they also practice a custom called "knocking of eggs." If a boy sees a girl he likes, he tries to knock his red colored egg against hers. She covers her egg to indicate disinterest, but if she likes him too, she allows their eggs to touch. The Chuang also have another custom called "making like old times." They dress up in period clothing and pretend to be people of ancient days so that those of the present day will learn about the past. On these occasions there is a colorful parade at night, illuminated by lanterns made in the shapes of animals and revolving carousels. It is accompanied by a lion dance to the sound of drums, horns, and firecrackers!

## THE HANI (Woni)

There are over half a million Hani (Woni) scattered around the southern part of Yunnan Province near the Hung Ho (Red River) where they share an autonomous district as well as a county with the Yi.

These primitive people plant terraced farms on the steep mountainside. Their region is extremely inaccessible, and they rely mainly on horses for transportation. Having no written language in the past, they used to record events by carving on wood.

Their holidays are celebrated with songs and dances as well as competitions in wrestling and marksmanship, since the Hani are excellent shots who make their own guns.

## THE KAWA

Only a few minorities of China, such as the Pulang and Kawa, living in the southwestern areas bordering Burma, Laos, and Vietnam, speak languages belonging to the Austroasiatic Family. The Kawa, whose population is estimated at 280,000, are concentrated in the mountainous regions of southwestern Yunnan Province.

With strong bonds of mutual help, the industrious and fearless Kawa practiced the "slash and burn"* method of farming, using implements of bamboo, wood, and stone until the 1950's. Productivity was so low that they had to rely partly on hunting and wild vegetables for food. Since then, irrigation, fertilizers, and other modern farming methods have greatly improved their standard of living.

Chieftains lead the Kawa in battle and hunting, but important matters are decided by the tribe in meetings where unanimous agreement is sought. Taboos abound. A stranger may not enter a village without first sending gifts to ask for permission. If salt or sugar cane comes back, a welcome is indicated; but pepper or tobacco means animosity and refusal. The bamboo houses of the Kawa have three entrances; the center one is reserved for supernatural beings and is used only at times of sacrificial offerings. The two side doors are for people and entrance to the garden.

Every village has a special house that is the gathering place for religious rituals. Inside are two wooden drums of different sizes, beaten by drummers using sticks of varying lengths to produce a scale of four notes. With variations in speed and rhythm, the

---

* This apparently is a primitive method by which the growth on a piece of virgin land is burned to the ground. The ashes provide fertilizer for the crop that is then planted in the clear ground. After the harvest, the land is abandoned and a new piece of virgin land has to be found for the next planting.

drummers can create distinctive musical compositions that serve the Kawa at times of sacrificial offering, war, and victory, as well as for dancing and recreation. The sound of drums is also a means of sending messages from village to village.

# THE KAZAKHS

The Slavic word for "Kazakh" is "Cossack," meaning a fugitive and masterless man. Kazakhs were independent nomadic herdsmen until the Russians conquered them in the nineteenth century. Today most of them live in the Kazakh Soviet Socialist Republic, but more than half a million are across the border in China—in Sinkiang, Tsinghai, and Kansu Provinces, with the greatest concentration in northern Sinkiang. Here they enjoy a mild climate and fertile soil as well as beautiful pastureland.

They are still nomads who tend sheep, goats, horses, cattle, and camels, although they also grow some grains and potatoes. Their diet is rich in dairy products such as milk and cheese. In the winter they live in permanent houses of earth and wood, but in the summer the Kazakhs camp in felt-covered tents that enable them to move about freely.

The Kazakhs are Muslims, but their women do not wear veils, and they are casual about observing religious rituals or dietary rules, with the exception of not eating pork. They are very tolerant of non-believers.

The Kazakhs are known for a musical instrument called the *dombra*, which has two strings and is plucked. Sometimes several varieties of this instrument are played together to create delightful harmonies. Kazakhs also love to sing songs that tell legends or folk tales. During holidays or festivities, a favorite pastime is a kind of singing contest in which groups of four (two men and two women), divided into two teams, match wits in making up lyrics to answer each other's words, the object being to overwhelm the opposite side. They may tease, or joke, or praise. When a guest comes to visit a Kazakh household, the women will find something special about the visitor and put their observations into a song. Shepherds sing impromptu tunes when they are inspired by their surroundings in the pastures. At funerals, singing is a means of expressing sorrow, while at weddings songs are joyously created under the stimulus of fermented mare's milk.

Like the neighboring Mongols, the Kazakhs are skilled horsemen, trained from childhood. They play a game of grabbing a sheep carcass from one another while riding on horses, awarding the sheep to the winner. Accompanied by dogs, they are also superb hunters on horseback, tracking down wolves and foxes whose fur pelts provide them with another source of income.

These carefree people are famous for their hospitality. When a stranger appears, be he of another tribe or language, the Kazakhs will invite him to stay the night and offer him specially prepared food and drink. If a family refuses lodging to a visitor, it will be reprimanded and criticized by the leaders of the community.


# THE KOREANS

The Koreans in China are an unassimilated minority with their own written and spoken languages. They number about 1.2 million and live mainly in the Yen-pien Korean Autonomous District and the Korean Autonomous County, both located in Kirin Province. Many came to China around 1870, when North Korea was struck by famine; others crossed the border in 1910 and the following years to escape the Japanese, who conquered and annexed Korea. But later, even Yen-pien fell under Japanese domination for some 14 years, when northeast China was ruled by the puppet regime of Manchukuo.

Most of the Koreans of Kirin are rice farmers, but an increasing number are entering the labor force of Manchuria, which is a highly industrialized part of China. Yen-pien produces lumber, metals, and minerals such as gold, silver, iron, coal, and oil shale.

Yen-pien is also known as the "Land of Song and Dance," for the lively and outgoing Koreans love to express their feelings through dancing and singing. They are athletic, too: the men enjoy football and wrestling and the girls play games of jumping on seesawing boards or gliding through the air on swings.

# THE LISU (LIZU)

About two-thirds of the 300,000 Lisu (Lizu) live in the northwest of Yunnan Province along three rivers: the Nu Chiang (Angry River), the Lan-ts'ang Chiang (Turbulent Blue River—also known as the Mekong), and the Chin-sha Chiang (Golden Sand River). However, earlier historical records for the T'ang dynasty (618–907 A.D.) indicate that they were natives of Szechuan, where some of them still remain. Apparently they kept migrating southward. By the Ch'ing dynasty (1644–1911 A.D.), a travel book mentioned the Lisu as hunting people in Yunnan. The Lisu near the Angry River tell stories of their move from the neighboring Golden Sand River.

These tales are handed down by oral tradition in songs and narrative poems. Songs are also a means of settling disputes or expressing sorrow over deaths; they are for recreation and celebrations and even for making bets. A favorite Lisu game is a song contest of questions and answers, wherein the loser must forfeit gifts to the winner.

Before the Communist revolution, the Lisu had no writing; they relied on incising wood to keep records. About 30 years ago Christian missionaries improvised a Latinized spelling for the native converts, but this system has been replaced by a new written language.

The Angry River Valley lies between two high mountains, one over 6000 meters above sea level and another over 4000 meters. The river rushes between these peaks with great turbulence, and the Lisu use a method of "sliding cable" to get across the chasm. Two strong stakes of uneven heights are driven into the ground on each shore; then bamboo cables (made of bamboo strips twisted together) connect the higher pole on one side with the lower one on the opposite. When a Lisu wishes to reach the other shore, he ties himself to a "sliding tube," holding on to it tightly. The tube is designed to slide over the bamboo cable. Lifting his feet off the ground, the traveler propels himself swiftly to about one-half the way across, at which point the momentum dies and he must use his arms and hands and feet to maneuver the rest of the way. Since the mountains are snowy, transportation is tremendously difficult, but in recent years steel cable bridges and highways have been built to replace these bamboo sliding bridges and the old mountain paths.

The climate in the Angry River district varies sharply; the valley is very hot, with a short frost season, and the southern part is suitable for planting semitropical crops. Mid-mountain, the weather is cool and pleasant, and most of the Lisu are found there. Higher, near the peaks, it is very cold and snowy all year round.

Rice is the Lisu staple, but they also grow corn, wheat, millet, kaoliang, and other grains. Their cash crops are hemp, lacquer- and tung-trees, and sugar cane. About 90 percent of the farms are terraced on the mountainside. The Lisu also gather plants in the forests of the high places for making some of the Chinese medicines most commonly used.

## THE MIAO

One of the largest minorities, the Miao number about 2,600,000 and are scattered widely. Nearly two million of them live in Kweichow, where they share an autonomous district with the Tung and another with the Puyi. The rest are found in other southwestern and southern provinces.

With no written language, the Miao used to rely on tying knots, incising bamboo, or counting colored beans for recording events or keeping accounts. They expressed their feelings in songs and epic poetry and sent messages via symbolic objects: a feather as a call for help, peppers as a sign of emergency, and tinder as a request for guns. Since 1956 a new written language has been devised.

The Miao believe in many supernatural beings, some of them ancestral ghosts and others spirits of nature. To these beings they perform long religious ceremonies that often involve magic and animal sacrifices. Nearly every village also has a shrine for the local earth god. The Miao believe that a person's soul leaves his body while he sleeps, and if an evil spirit lures it away, the individual may become ill. In death, the soul rises to the sky, some souls may turn into evil spirits.

In Kweichow Province many live in settlements on mountain slopes, and the villages are surrounded by mud or stone walls. The interiors of their houses are separated by pillars rather than walls.

As there is little arable land on the slopes, the Miao practice the "slash and burn" method of farming. Corn and various other grains and beans are planted on the high ground, and wet rice is the chief crop on the lower levels and near the riverbanks. Cash crops include tea, tung-seed oil, tobacco, sugar cane, and indigo. Besides farming, handicrafts such as bamboo mats, hats, boxes, fishtraps, or cloth woven at home also bring some income. The women embroider flowers, birds, and animals in a great variety of designs over coarse gauzes or silks and satins, and the men work at silversmithing, blacksmithing, and carpentry.

Most of the Miao marry early—about the age of 17 or 18—and are monogamous, but some men keep concubines in separate households. There is considerable sexual freedom among the unmarried. During periods of leisure from agricultural activities, young men will band together to roam from village to village and assemble on the courting slope. There they will commence to woo the girls by whistling tunes on leaves held between their lips, and the women respond by coming out and grouping themselves on another side of the slope. Thus, standing or squatting, the two sexes sing to each other, ending with each boy choosing a girl and asking her permission for a chat. If she consents, the couple will sit near each other and start a conversation of ordinary small talk mixed with singing. If they do not hit it off, they will go their separate ways after an hour or two and look for other partners, but if they like each other, this is a prelude to courtship and marriage.

The wedding usually takes place around the First or Second Moon. It is customary for the groom and his friends to come to the girl's village to escort her to the boy's village, arriving there by night, and the neighbors pour out with lighted torches to look at the prospective bride, the women admiring her clothing and the men jesting to make her smile. However, the marriage is not yet consummated. After 13 days the bride returns to her parents and waits for the groom to send for her to help with the work during the busy season. This time, the two begin housekeeping together as man and wife.

Besides the New Year, the Miao celebrate several other festivals. One interesting holiday is the "Rice Eating Among Sisters" on the 16th day of the Fourth Moon. This is in memory of two sisters who were forced by circumstances to part and shared a meal of rice before their separation. On this holiday, the women put on festive clothing and jewelry and gather for parties and dancing.

Another colorful occasion is the Dragon Boat Festival, which falls soon after the planting of rice and lasts from the 24th to the 28th of the Fifth Moon. Unlike the Han holiday of the same name, which is in memory of a poet, the Miao version is based on a legend about a dragon king who kidnaped the child of a fisherman. The fisherman burned the dragon king, causing thick smoke to cover the sky for 9 days and 9 nights. Later, a child playing by the river called "Tung! tung! tung!" and the sky suddenly cleared up. Ever since, the sound of gongs and drums are an integral part of the Dragon Boat races at this celebration.

## THE MONGOLS

The Mongols in China are of Central Asian origin. They number over 1,600,000, and more than a million of them live in the Inner Mongolian Autonomous Region. The rest are scattered over northeast and northwest China.

As the climate of Inner Mongolia is dry and there are grassy pastures for grazing, most Mongols are nomadic herdsmen who live in camps, called *bok*, made up of several tents. If the *bok* has to move around freely, the tents are constructed with a center pole and covered with dark cotton cloth; but if the camp can stay in one place longer, *yurts* may take the place of tents. *Yurts* are built by covering a lattice framework with felt, secured by ropes. A hole in the roof lets out smoke from cooking and heating. The average *yurt* is about 3 or 4 meters in diameter and, in addition to a stove, contains a Buddhist altar, two beds, and two cabinets. A large *yurt* may hold more than ten beds. The Mongols store their extra food, clothing, and even jewelry in carts, which are boxes on wheels, so that they can move their belongings to a new location at a moment's notice!

The livelihood of the Mongols depends on their animals— sheep, cattle, horses, and camels. Their favorite meat is lamb, and they also consume many dairy products such as milk, cheese, and cream. They drink fermented cow's or mare's milk somewhat as we drink wine. Animal skins and wool provide the raw material for clothing. Because of their dependence on horses for locomotion, Mongols are trained to be horsemen from a very early age, so that even little children as well as old women can ride with amazing skill and speed. Camels are another means of transportation, especially as beasts of burden, for they can carry heavy weights and travel for long periods in the desert without drinking water.

Since early times the Mongol culture has been influenced by other people. From the Tibetans they acquired Lamaist Buddhism as their religion, and from the Han Chinese they adopted an administrative and governmental system. Their economy was affected by the Han people who immigrated into Mongolia. When the population pressure was great, the Mongols sometimes moved to freer areas of the steppes. Some of them also traded animals and products with the Han. The poorer ones even took up farming and lived among them. In recent years, the Mongolian class structure was dismantled by the Communists, who introduced the commune and state farms.

Around June or July, the Mongols enjoy their yearly rest. They take advantage of the fine summer weather to celebrate, featuring wrestling and competitions in horsemanship during these holidays. Other favorite Mongolian pastimes are music and storytelling. When a storyteller sings his tales accompanied by his fiddle, Mongols come on horseback from hundreds of miles to listen to his verses.


## THE NUNG

Ever since the 8th century the Chuang minority rebelled against Chinese imperial rule. In 1059 one of their leaders, named Nung

Chih Kao, established the Kingdom of Nan Tien (the Kingdom of Southern Heaven) in present day Yunnan Province, but he was ultimately defeated by a Sung general. The Nung people are probably the descendants of Nung Chih Kao.

## THE ORONCHON

There are only about 3000 Oronchon, and they live chiefly in Inner Mongolia and Heilungkiang, a province that is part of Manchuria. The Oronchon are a Tungusic people; therefore they are related to the Manchus who ruled China for nearly 300 years (Ch'ing dynasty, 1644–1911 A.D.). Banded together in tribes of several dozen to a hundred, they are excellent horsemen and marksmen. In the past, an Oronchon's livelihood depended almost entirely on a horse, a gun, and a hunting dog, and the principal game was red deer. They ate meat and made clothing out of animal skins. Their houses were primitive conical tents built with 20 or 30 wooden poles.

Oronchon have many superstitions and taboos. For example, a woman must give birth in a tent separate from the living quarter. To see a dog with drooping tail is bad luck; it portends sickness. But they are also a brave and hardy people who dearly prize their freedom. During the Japanese occupation of Manchuria, they resisted and fought fiercely.

Today the Chinese government has set aside autonomous areas for the Oronchon and is helping them to build permanent houses and learn farming as a means of livelihood. Because of this, the Oronchon are forsaking their former nomadic hunting life and are beginning to settle down.

## THE PAI

The Pai, formerly called "Min-chia," are believed to have been originally natives of the Yangtze River Valley, the culture of which came under Chinese influence early in history. About 2000 years ago they migrated southward due to the pressure of Han expansion and settled in the northwest of Yunnan Province near Erh Hai Lake. There they conquered the Kingdom of Nan-chao after 937 A.D. and established the Kingdom of Tali. Today some 680,000 Pai live in Yunnan, concentrated near Tali by the Erh Hai or farther north. Tali is one of the most scenic spots of China. Known as the "Switzerland of the East," it enjoys a climate noted for azure skies and crisp air. It is blessed with clear lakes and rivers, and its majestic mountains are famous for the marble with which they abound. The Pai are excellent stonemasons.

Early in the T'ang dynasty (618–907 A.D.), Buddhism came to the Pai people. One of the mountains on the eastern shore of Erh Hai is dotted with over 50 temples, which in the ancient past were often visited by monks from India and Burma.

Large families consisting of several generations who live together are the norm for the Pai, but there are smaller families. Like the Han, the Pai observe a taboo against marriage between persons with the same family name, but favor cousin alliances that do not fall into this category.

The Pai excel in sculpture and painting. Pao Shih Shan, or Gem Stone Mountain, is famous for its 9th to 11th century sculptures portraying royalty. Around 1240 a Pai artist named Chang Sheng-wen completed a scroll depicting the meeting of a Tali king with Buddhas and rulers of the sixteen kingdoms of India. Nearly 60 feet long, this celebrated handscroll portraying hundreds of characters is now in the National Palace Museum of Taipei.

Pai literature is rich in folk tales and poetry, with narrative songs that tell the story of the creation and origin of mankind. Music is so much a part of daily life that parental education is often rated according to the number of songs taught to the children. In recreation and celebrations, everyone is expected to take part in singing contests.

During the Torch Festival on the 25th of the Sixth Moon, pine branches and dry twigs are piled around a large evergreen decorated with bamboos, flowers, and strings of fruits and goodies. After supper, the villagers tie wheat stalks and reeds into the shape of brooms and gather around the tree. Then they light their torches and set the evergreen on fire, scrambling to grab as many prizes dropping from the tree as they can. They believe a person who gets many sweets and cakes will have a new son in the coming year, while one whose booty consists of flowers will have a beautiful daughter. As the celebration continues, the people swat one another with their smoldering torches to beat out all illnesses, bad luck, and impurities.

## THE PUYI (Chung-chia)

Among the ten largest minorities in China, the Puyi live almost entirely in Kweichow Province, concentrating along the Hung-shui Ho (Red Water River) and its tributary near the border of Kwangsi Province. Numbering about 1,300,000, scholars believe they were originally the same people as the Chuang, but gradually lost contact and became a separate ethnic group. Since 1956 they have been sharing an autonomous district with the Miao.

The Puyi are so much under the influence of Han culture that it is often difficult to distinguish them, although older women still wear the traditional tight jackets and long skirts. They have adopted the Han language in place of the Tai spoken by their ancestors, and many of them are literate.

The Puyi live in an area blessed with mild climate and fertile soil, but salt is deficient here and goiters are a common affliction. Most Puyi are moderately rich farmers who grow rice and corn, legumes and other vegetables as well as sugar cane and tobacco. A few live in towns and engage in trade. Since their territory is rich in mineral resources such as iron, antimony, coal, and lead, industry and mining are being introduced rapidly.

## THE SHUI (Shui-chia)

Called "Shui-chia" in the past, the Shui are one of the more prominent minorities with a long history. Their present population is estimated to be around 160,000. Most Shui have lived in southeast Kweichow for more than a thousand years, although some are also found in Kwangsi Province. About the year 1855 they participated in the T'ai-p'ing Rebellion that almost overthrew the Manchu dynasty—an act attesting to their independent spirit. The Shui language is related to that of the Tung and has a hieroglyphic writing. They also have their own calendar, the first month of which falls on the Ninth Moon of the Chinese lunar calendar.

Shui settlements of small wooden houses are located in beautiful surroundings of mountains and rivers; the lower floor of the houses is used for storage and animals, and the upper levels for living. There are three public areas in each village: a slope for racing horses, a hall for dancing and singing, and another slope for lovers. In clothing, the Shui favor shades of blue, and the women wear their hair coiled on top of the head, decorated with a silver comb.

In addition to farming, handicraft is an important occupation. The women are skillful at weaving and embroidery, and the villagers produce charming paper cuttings and sculptures.

Every year in the fall, drums are sounded and houses cleaned for the celebration of the harvest festival. Wearing new clothing for the occasion, the villagers cook just-picked glutinous rice and a chowder of fresh fish. The celebrations include a horse race on the slope, with a leading citizen opening the ceremony by circling the racing area on horseback. To the beating of drums the people improvise songs in praise of the harvest, admired individuals, and lucky events.


## THE TAI

The Thai of present-day Thailand originated from the Tai of China. Today the Tai number more than half a million and live in Yunnan Province. They and a few other minorities, namely the large Chuang group, the Puyi, Tung, and Shui, speak dialects classified as northern Tai, whereas the dialects spoken outside China belong to a southwestern branch.

The Chinese Tai have no written language of their own, but some of them use the Shan alphabet of the Burmese, while others borrow that of the southwestern dialects. Both these systems of writing derive from Indian sources, and the Chinese government is trying to help the Tai perfect them.

Buddhism is the religion of the Tai in China as well as of the Thai in Thailand. We know that 400 years ago the Tai already had a city of more than 10,000 families that boasted over 200 temples. Today every village has at least one, sometimes two, temples. These places of worship are decorated with murals of religious paintings and festooned with banners that hang from the ceiling. Inside and around the grounds are sacred *bodi* trees that no one may harm.

Built on stilts, Tai houses are mostly two-story pavilions with verandas, made of bamboo, although in the cities it is possible to find one-story buildings. Roofs are usually thatched, but sometimes tiled. The lower floor is used for storage and animals as well as grain mills and looms for weaving. Tai people regard house-building as a community activity; they do not need to hire contractors, but simply invite their friends and relatives, who pitch in to build a house in short order.

As there is plenty of rain and the soil is very fertile, the principal occupation is agriculture, rice being the most important crop. Many tropical fruits such as bananas, coconuts, pineapples, lichees and papayas are also grown, while camphor, rubber, quinine, coffee and a famous *p'u-erh* tea bring ready cash to the economy.

The Tai are creative craftsmen who weave brocades out of silk and metallic threads, shape elegant pottery, and fashion exquisite silver betel boxes whose designs are of Indian origin.

They have their own calendar, which is two months ahead of the Chinese lunar calendar and 638 years behind the Julian calendar of the West. For example, the year 1979 is the Tai year 1341. Around the middle of the Han's Fourth Moon (the Sixth to the Tai), just before the start of the rainy season, the Tai celebrate the Water Sprinkling Festival. The legend goes that once a cruel demon was tricked by the youngest of his seven wives into revealing that he had a mysterious white hair, which, when pulled, could kill him. She plucked out the hair and laid it across his throat, decapitating and killing him; but flames shot up from his blood and other demons sprang out all around. The oldest wife was brave enough to pick up the severed head and wrap it in red cloth, thus putting out the flames and making the demons disappear. From then on, the wives dared not put down the bundle, but took turns holding it for a year. On each anniversary, they sprinkled water to cleanse it and themselves. Today the Water Sprinkling Festival is a holiday on which the Tai wish one another good health and long life. They also like to sing and dance on other occasions, and these songs and dances deal with cheerful themes such as the joys of daily life and of nature. They have hunting dances, elephant-foot drum dances, and peacock dances.

## THE TIBETANS

There are about 3 million Tibetans in China, more than a million living in the Tibetan Autonomous Region on the high mountains and plateaus of the Himalaya Range. The rest are scattered in Tsinghai, Szechuan, Kansu, and Yunnan Provinces.

Most Tibetans are farmers living in villages ruled by elected chieftains and a council of elders. About 20 percent are nomadic herdsmen who live in camps of 5 to 80 families, which move to higher and higher pastures during the summer to take advantage of the short growing season on each level. In the winter they come down into the valley to make a living by trading, repairing equipment, and weaving cloth.

The marriage customs of the Tibetans are different from ours. A man can have several wives or only one, and a woman may also have several husbands. Before Tibet came under Communist rule, the oldest son was the only one who had the right to marry. When he had a child, he replaced his father as the head of the family. His younger brothers usually entered monasteries. But if the oldest brother had no son, one of the others might come back to take his place as head of the family and live with the oldest son's wife without getting married.

The state religion of Tibet is Lamaism, a form of Buddhism.

The lamas, or priests, used to be very powerful, but their influence has become greatly reduced and many have returned to lay life.

The main staple in Tibetan diet is barley, dried under the sun, ground into flour, mixed with butter and strong tea, and shaped into dumplings. Beef and lamb are common meats, and a special beverage is "buttered tea" made by brewing brick tea and adding butter and salt to it. On special occasions, colored buttered dough is shaped into flowers, people, landscapes, and architecture for decoration or religious offerings—an ingenious art form suitable only for the winter!

There are three kinds of Tibetan dwellings. Nomadic tents are made of felt, a wood pole, and ropes, easily set up and dismantled. Village houses are built of mud, bricks, or stones and may be one to three stories high. If the house has three stories, the first is for cattle, horses or storage, the second for kitchen and living quarters, and the third for a Buddhist altar and worship. The third type of house is the lama temple. These temples may be truly imposing structures set into the mountainside, such as the temple in Lhasa, which boasts thirteen stories and is 100 meters in height.

Tibetan festivals are related to agriculture and religion. New Year's Eve is celebrated by feasting and changing window and door drapery to symbolize newness. On New Year's Day, friends exchange ceremonial scarves and there is dancing in the streets. On the 15th day, a lantern festival ends the New Year holidays. The 15th day of the Fourth Moon is devoted to praying for good harvest and the remembrance of Buddha's birth and death. On the 15th day of the Fifth Moon, dancing and singing outdoors celebrate the coming of good crops. Horse races liven up the summer, while harvest festivals gladden the autumn. On the 25th day of the Tenth Moon, the Tibetans pray and light lamps in memory of the passing of Tsong-ka-pa, the founder of their religion.

Tibetans love the theater. Actors sing their parts, echoed by choruses. Lion and yak dances are also very popular, the lion dance being very much like the ones we see in Chinatown. These artistic people make fine carved utensils and furniture and weave beautiful fabrics and rugs. Their religious paintings and gilt bronze sculptures are highly prized and collected by museums all over the world.

# T'UCHIA

The name "T'uchia" means "native." There are about 600,000 T'uchia people in China, living in Hunan and Hupei Provinces as well as in Szechuan and Kweichow. Nearly four hundred thousand of them are concentrated in the western part of Hunan, intermingling and sharing an autonomous district with the Miao minority. The Tuchia are the original inhabitants of this region and they refer to the Han majority around them as "guests."

Living in a mountainous area, they grow rice on terraced farms and plant tung trees (from whose seeds tung oil—an important Chinese export—is extracted), as well as vegetables and fruit trees. They have long been under Han cultural influence, but dress somewhat differently, the women covering their hair with hats or cloth wrapping and the men wearing jackets that have many fasteners down the middle. T'uchia women are known for their skill in weaving a kind of native cloth of beautiful design that is used for making bedrolls.

Epic poetry is a part of their literary heritage. The narratives deal with the creation of the world and mankind as well as with the origin of the tribe, its migrations, and the exploits of ancient heroes. Some of these epics have been translated into the Han language. Other oral literature such as songs, stories, and drama are also being recorded in writing.

The T'uchia have a native dance called "Hand Waving Dance." Every new year around the 3rd to the 15th of the First Moon, they gather in front of the temple of the local god and dance to drums and gongs, acting out the events of the year, which are concerned for the most part with their farming and hunting activities.

# THE TUNG

About 820,000 Tung people live in an area where Kweichow, Hunan, and Kwangsi Provinces meet. More than half of them are in Kweichow, and there are autonomous Tung districts and counties in all three provinces. Speaking a Sino-Tibetan language, they had no writing until recently.

The Tung are talented architects. They live in houses built on stilts with roofs of tiles or wooden shingles. These are two or three stories high, with the lowest level reserved for domestic animals. Legend tells of a brother and sister in ancient times who escaped a great flood inside a gourd. After the deluge they got married but had no home, and a swallow brought them seeds from which they grew trees. With the wood from the trees they built a house off the ground to avoid future floods and invited the swallow to live on the beam. Later, more floors were added, so they moved upstairs and kept animals below, but the house remains on stilts to this day.

The Tung also fashion a kind of "coiled dragon bridge" by piling mounds of stones in the river over which wooden beams are laid. Then planks are placed across the beams for flooring. Corridors and pavilions, with ceilings exquisitely painted or carved, are erected over the bridge, the whole structure put together with mortise and tenon without using a single nail. These bridges serve not only as passageways over rivers and streams, but also as protection against the weather. Benches are provided for resting, and fresh spring water and new straw sandals offered free of charge.

One of the villages has a drum tower taller than any other building. When some momentous event occurs, the drum is sounded to summon the people for a meeting.

However, Tung creativity is not limited to architecture. Music played on reed pipes and lutes and colorful dances of great variety are a part of daily life; singing is an indispensable part of courtship. Folk tales and drama, formerly handed down orally, are now being recorded in writing. The Tung women learn to embroider from childhood and produce works of great beauty without having to make preliminary sketches. They weave a fine cloth that resembles satin.


# THE UIGHURS

Uighurs are a large Central Asian minority who speak a Turkic language. Estimated at 5 million, they live in the southern two thirds of Sinkiang. Since the Tien Shan Mountains cut across the vast province and act as a screen shielding the Tarim Basin in the south from cold north winds, this part of Sinkiang is warm and dry. Many oases in the desert make farming possible for the Uighurs, who plant garden crops, winter wheat, corn, and rice as well as cotton for cash. They are also famous for their luscious fruits: melons, grapes, peaches, and apricots. In addition, they raise silkworms and keep cattle, horses, sheep, and camels, but they are not nomadic and live in settled communities.

As the Uighurs need human labor for irrigating the crops, they prize large families. Several generations, including married children, often live under one roof. If a woman is childless she is despised.

Uighurs use an Arabic script and consider themselves Muslims, but they do not observe religious rituals or dietary rules strictly. They have also retained some native beliefs in ghosts and spirits, and consult witch doctors when they are sick.

Men and women wear colorful embroidered or beaded caps and hats, often trimmed with fur in the winter. The wide sleeves and graceful pleated skirts of the women make them look like butterflies fluttering their wings. Uighurs also wear leather shoes or boots, and padded garments when the weather is cold. The staple foods are wheat and corn and a good deal of roast lamb. Another favorite is rice cooked with meats, carrots, duck eggs, butter, and onions. It is fragrant and delicious and is eaten with the fingers.

Uighurs love to dance and sing. They have song cycles handed down by oral tradition from ancient times, and some of their dances are performed without music—known as "pure dance."

In the summer they like to hold picnics under the trees and in the winter there are parties of dancing, singing, and storytelling. Festivals are celebrated with music and games, such as trying to grab a slaughtered lamb from an opponent while riding on horseback, or competitions in bodily strength. Once a week the market is a place where people come not only to buy and sell, but to enjoy the carnival atmosphere; sometimes tens of thousands will gather from miles around. The merchandise ranges from beaded caps, hand-woven cloths, daggers, medicines, and boots to a wide variety of foods such as roast meat, cold noodles, ice cream, sour milk, and breads. These occasions are noisy and joyous, filled with the sounds of laughter, singing, and musical instruments.

## THE YI

Sometimes called "Lolo," the Yi are a large minority numbering nearly 3½ million. More than a million live on the border between Szechuan and Yunnan Provinces in the Liang Shan (Cool Mountain) district. Others are found inside Yunnan as well as in Kweichow and Kwangsi Provinces.

The Yi are an agricultural people who plant corn and wheat in addition to beans and buckwheat and some potatoes, vegetables, and rice. They used to practice the "slash and burn" method, which was very wasteful of land and harmful to the soil, but more modern ways are taking over. Terrace farming is making efficient use of their rough terrain. The Yi live in mud houses surrounded by mud walls and keep their horses and oxen within the enclosures. They wear turbans and long woolen overcoats.

Before the Communist revolution, the Yi had a rigid caste system. The ruling class was called "Black Yi." They belonged to clans who owned all the land, sometimes spreading over several villages. Although agriculture was of prime importance to their economy, the Black Yi did not consider farming a suitable occupation for themselves. Instead, they preferred herding and left the planting and harvesting to the White Yi, a lower caste who also served as domestics. If a Black Yi had more land than he needed, he could rent it to a White Yi, who then became his tenant farmer and paid a large percentage of his crops as rent. Below both the Black and White Yi there were captured Han and other people who were slaves. A slave could eventually intermarry with the White Yi and become one, but the White Yi and Black Yi were forbidden to marry each other and there was no social mobility between them. Because it was so important to belong to a clan, there was much inbreeding. A Yi could marry the widow of his brother or even of his uncle or nephew. In that way, family ties were maintained and the high "bride price" was not wasted.

Yi have their own written language, but it was used only by the priests; the rest of the population was illiterate. They believe in a destiny controlled by good and bad spirits, so fortune-telling and the wearing of amulets to ward off evil are important. Their religious leaders act as sorcerers and medicine men. All this has begun to change since the Communist revolution.

Excellent hunters, the Yi catch their prey by using spears, guns and the crossbow as well as traps, nets, and drugs. They enjoy wrestling, which is a necessary part of wedding celebrations. Representatives of the bride and of the groom engage each other in competition, sometimes deliberately losing to the opponent in order to show friendship. Another favorite activity is dancing. Stomping on the ground by a roaring fire to the accompaniment of three-stringed instruments and short flutes, the Yi will sing and dance from evening to dawn.

A famous holiday is the Torch Festival, which takes place on the 24th day of the Sixth Moon. The festival originally commemorated Yi heroes who defeated an enemy, but it has gradually become a fertility rite. A long parade of torches snakes through the dark night to the music of reed pipes, sheepskin drums, brass gongs, and the tooting of horns. Girls play on four-stringed guitars while young men sing bawdy songs. The festival concludes as the chieftain presides over the selection of mates. Those who are not chosen must blow out their torches and return home to wait for next year's festival.


# CLASSIFICATION OF PRINCIPAL
# ETHNIC GROUPS BY LANGUAGES

SINO-TIBETAN FAMILY
    *Han** (majority)

    *Hui*

    *Tibeto-Burman:*
                Tibetan*
                Ch'iang*
                Yi (Lolo)*
                Pai (Min-chia)*
                T'uchia*

Hani (Woni)*
Lisu (Lizu)*
Chingpo
Lahu
Nasi

*Tai:*

Puyi (Chung-chia)*
Tung*
Tai*
Chuang* (also Nung*—probably related
     to Chuang)
Shui (Shui-chia)*

*Miao-Yao:*

Miao*
Yao
She


# ALTAIC FAMILY

*Turkic:*

Uighur*
Kazakh*
Kirghiz
Salar
Uzbek

*Mongolian:*

Mongol*
Tung-hsiang
Tu (Mongor)
Daur

*Tungusic:*

Oronchon*
Sibo
Evenki

*Korean*

AUSTROASIATIC FAMILY

Mon-Khmer:
Kawa*
Pulang (Puman)

INDO-EUROPEAN FAMILY

Tadzhik

* Represented by stories in this book.

# BIBLIOGRAPHY

1. Bonnet, Leslie, *Chinese Fairy Tales*, Frederick Muller, London, 1966.
2. Carpenter, Frances, *Tales of a Chinese Grandmother*, Doubleday, New York, 1946.
3. Central Intelligence Agency, *People's Republic of China Atlas*, U.S. Government Printing Office, Washington, D.C., 1971.
4. Central Institute for National Minorities, ed. by, *Shao-shu Min-tsu Shih-ko Hsüan* [Selections from the Poetry and Songs of Minority Nationalities], People's Literature Publishing House, Peking, 1975.
5. Chang, Ch'i-yün and Chu, Ko-chen, ed. *Pen-kuo Ti-li* [National Geography], 2 vols, Commercial Press, Shanghai, 1935.
6. Chen Wen, ed., *Chung-kuo Min-chien Ku-shih* [Chinese Folk Tales], v. 2 of 2 vols, Kuo-kuang Book Co., Hongkong, 1977.

7. Chia, Chih and Sun, Chien-ping, ed., *Chung-kuo Min-chien Ku-shih Hsüan* [Selections of Chinese Folk Tales], v. 1, People's Literature Publishing House, Peking, 1962.

8. Chin, Ching-yü, Ling, Ta-hsia and Chin, Chu-an, *Chung-hua Jen-min Kung-ho-kuo Fen-sheng Ti-tu* [People's Republic of China Atlas by Provinces], Ya-kuang Yü-ti Hsüeh-she, Shanghai, Peking, Canton, Hankow, Nanking, 1951.

9. *China's Minority Nationalities—Selected Articles from Chinese Sources*, Red Sun Publishers, San Francisco, 1977.

10. *Chung-kuo Tung-wu Ku-shih Chi* [Collection of Chinese Animal Stories], Shanghai Literature and Arts Publishing House, Shanghai, 1962.

11. Eberhard, Wolfram, *A History of China*, University of California Press, Berkeley and Los Angeles, 1960.

12. Eberhard, Wolfram, *Chinese Fairy Tales and Folk Tales*, E. P. Dutton & Co., New York, 1938.

13. Eberhard, Wolfram, *Chinese Festivals*, Henry Schuman, New York, 1952.

14. Eberhard, Wolfram, ed., *Folktales of China*, Washington Square Press, Simon and Schuster, New York, 1973.

15. Fairbank, John K., Reischauer, Edwin O., and Craig, Albert M., *East Asia—The Modern Transformation*, Houghton Mifflin Co., Boston, 1965.

16. Fairservis, Walter A., Jr., *Costumes of the East*, Published in Association with the American Museum of Natural History, The Chatham Press, Riverside, Conn., 1971.

17. Goodrich, L. Carrington, *A Short History of the Chinese People*, George Allen and Unwin Ltd., London, 1969.

18. Granet, Marcel, *Festivals and Songs of Ancient China*, E. P. Dutton & Co., New York, 1932.

19. Hsi, Kao, *Walo Hamlet*, Foreign Language Press, Peking, 1977.

20. Hsiao, Chung-yu, ed., *Chung-kuo Min-chien Ku-shih* [Chinese Folk Tales], vol. 1 of 2 vols., Kuo-kuang Book Co., Hongkong, 1977.

21. Hsieh, Chiao-min and Salter, Christopher L., ed., *Atlas of China*, McGraw Hill, 1973.

22. *Hsiung-ti Min-tsu Hsing-hsiang Fu-shih Tzu-liao* [Material on Costumes and Appearances of Brother Nationalities], 5 vols., Kwangsi Chuang Autonomous Region, 1976.

23. Kendall, Carol and Li, Yao-wen, *Sweet and Sour—Tales from China Retold*, The Bodley Head, London, Sydney, Toronto, 1979.

24. Kuo, Louis and Yuan-hsi, *Chinese Folk Tales*, Celestial Arts, Millbrae, Calif., 1976.

25. Reischauer, Edwin O. and Fairbank, John K., *East Asia—The Great Tradition*, Houghton Mifflin Co., Boston, 1960.

26. Shanghai Normal College, Department of Geography, ed., *Tsu-kuo-ti Hao Shan-ho* [The Wonderful Mountains and Rivers of Our Country], Shanghai People's Publishing House, Shanghai, 1973.

27. Smith, Bradley and Weng, Wan-go, *China—A History in Art*, Doubleday, New York, 1978.

28. Sung, Che, ed., *Chi-lin Min-chien Ku-shih* [Folk Tales from Kirin], The Won Yit Book Co., Hongkong, 1962.

29. Sung, Che, ed., *Heilungkiang Min-chien Ku-shih* [Folk Tales from Heilungkiang], The Won Yit Book Co., Hongkong, 1962.

30. Sung, Che, ed., *Hsi-tsang Min-chien Ku-shih* [Folk Tales from Tibet], The Won Yit Book Co., Hongkong, 1962.

31. Sung, Che, ed., *Hunan Min-chien Ku-shih* [Folk Tales from Hunan], The Won Yit Book Co., Hongkong, 1962.

32. Sung, Che, ed., *Kweichow Min-chien Ku-shih* [Folk Tales from Kweichow], The Won Yit Book Co., Hongkong, 1962.

33. Sung, Che, ed., *Shantung Min-chien Ku-shih* [Folk Tales from Shantung], The Won Yit Book Co., Hongkong, 1962.

34. Sung, Che, ed., *Yunnan Min-chien Ku-shih* [Folk Tales from Yunnan], 2 vols., The Won Yit Book Co., Hongkong, 1961.

35. Tan, Hsin-chih, ed., *Chung-kuo Shao-shu Min-tsu Hsin-mao* [The New Look of Chinese Minorities], Shanghai Book Co., Hongkong, 1976.

36. Ting Tang, ed., *Chung-kuo Min-tsu Wu* [Chinese Folk Dances], The I-ch'ün Publishing Co., Hongkong, 1975.

37. Werner, E.T.C., *A Dictionary of Chinese Mythology*, The Julian Press, New York, 1961.

38. Werner, E.T.C., *Myths and Legends of China*, George G. Harrap & Co., London, Toronto, Wellington, Sydney, 1958.

39. Whitaker, Donald P. and Shinn, Rinn-Sup, with Barth, Helen A., Heimann, Judith M., MacDonald, John E., Martindale,

Kenneth W. and Weaver, John O., *Area Handbook for the People's Republic of China*, U.S. Government Printing Office, Washington, D.C., 1972.

40. Yin Ming, *United and Equal—The Progress of China's Minority Nationalities*, Foreign Language Press, Peking, 1977.

*41. *Zhonghua Renmin Gongheguo Fen Sheng Dituji* [People's Republic of China Atlas by Provinces—Chinese Pinyin Edition], Ditu Chubanshe, Beijing, 1977. (*Transliteration of Chinese names by Pinyin System)

Note: Transliterations of proper names and place names in our book are based upon the Wade-Giles system. For Pinyin versions of geographical names, please refer to Item #41 of the bibliography.

# 中国民间故事选

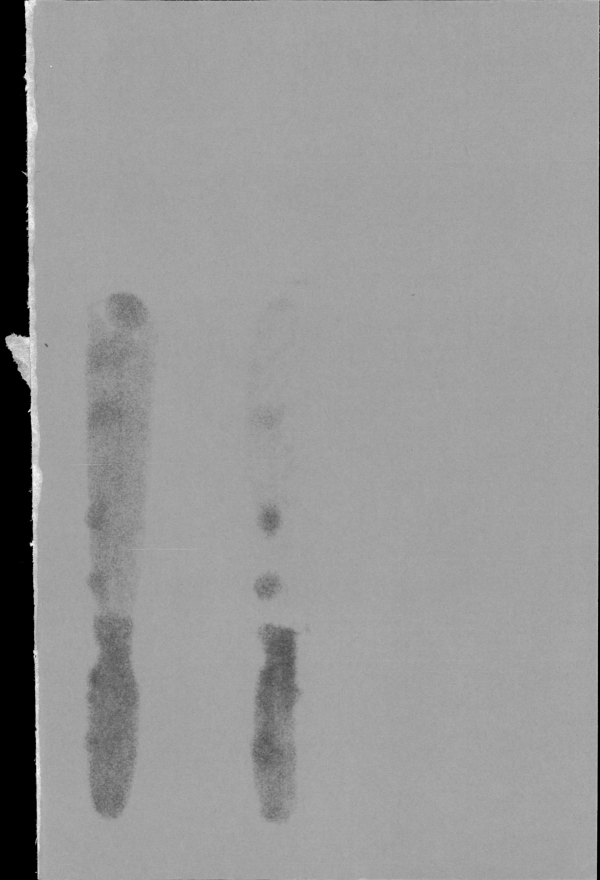

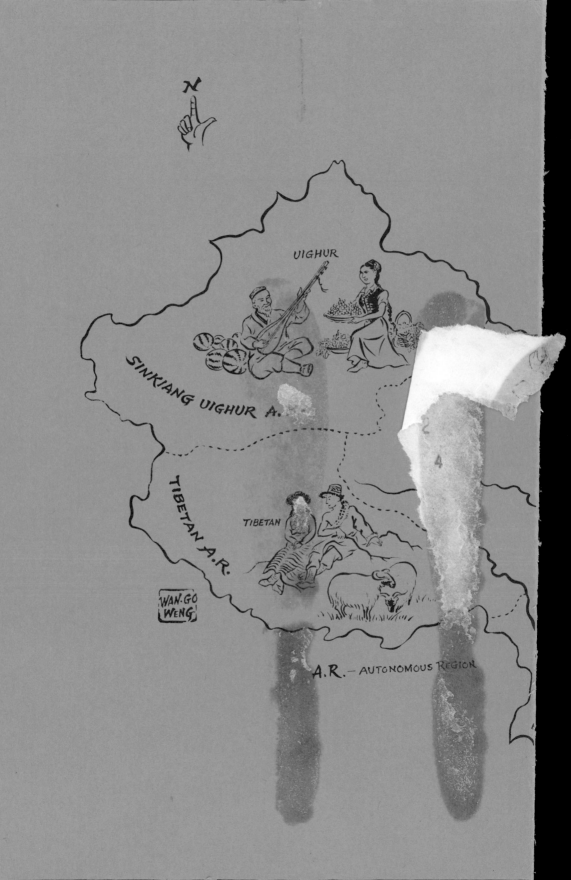

N

UIGHUR

SINKIANG UIGHUR A.

TIBETAN A.R.

TIBETAN

WAN-GO
WENG

A.R. — AUTONOMOUS REGION